Market Values
in American
Higher Education

Market Values in American Higher Education

The Pitfalls and Promises

Charles W. Smith

ROWMAN & LITTLEFIELD PUBLISHERS, INC.
Lanham • Boulder • New York • Oxford

ROWMAN & LITTLEFIELD PUBLISHERS, INC.

Published in the United States of America
by Rowman & Littlefield Publishers, Inc.
4720 Boston Way, Lanham, Maryland 20706
http://www.rowmanlittlefield.com

12 Hid's Copse Road, Cumnor Hill, Oxford OX2 9JJ, England

British Library Cataloging in Publication Information Available

Library of Congress Cataloging-in-Publication Data

Smith, Charles W., 1938–
  Market values in American higher education : the pitfalls and promises / Charles W. Smith.
    p. cm.
  Includes bibliographical references and index.
  ISBN 0-8476-9563-8 (cloth : alk. paper)—ISBN 0-8476-9564-6 (paper : alk. paper)
  1. Education, Higher—United States—Finance. 2. College costs—United States.
  3. Education, Higher—Economic aspects—United States. I. Title.
LB2342.S55 2000
338.4'337873—dc21   99-089685

Printed in the United States of America

♾™ The paper used in this publication meets the minimum requirements of American National Standard for Information Sciences—Permanence of Paper for Printed Library Materials, ANSI/NISO Z39.48-1992.

*To my teachers, colleagues, and students,
who contributed to this book in innumerable ways.*

Contents

Preface and Acknowledgments

The thesis of this book is quite simple. Market principles have been, and continue to be, misapplied to American higher education, causing significant economic inefficiencies and undermining the educational process. My argument has three parts: One, that the widespread criticism of fiscal and personnel mismanagement leveled against higher education's traditional way of doing business is wrongheaded. Two, that nearly all of the remedial economic/market actions recommended and taken to correct these assumed inefficiencies have proven counterproductive, wasting and misusing existing resources, increasing costs, and causing widespread harm. My third point follows directly from the second point. Real economic efficiencies require building on traditional academic management and governance structures, which prove to be implicitly highly market sensitive, rather than destroying them.

All three of these factors are rooted in a pervasive failure to appreciate not only the singular, economically efficient character of American higher education, but also the limitations of what might be called hierarchical corporate management structures in educational settings. In short, the problem isn't with the traditional fiscal and organizational structure of higher education, but with inappropriate and destructive models that numerous critics of American higher education have sought to impose on higher education. On the other hand, I should stress that I am not arguing that economic efficiencies and market principles have no place in American higher education. The problem does not lie with accountability and market principles per se, but with the naïve way these principles have been interpreted and applied within the educational context.

Because of the widespread public concern with the increased cost of higher education and the ongoing public debates regarding the causes for this phenomenon, I have elected to write this book for a general audience of

ix

concerned readers. I have consequently limited the types of complex financial analyses that support my basic argument and replace them with more
concrete examples and analogies. I have included references to supporting
materials in notes. I have also attempted to avoid becoming involved in what
is commonly referred to as the culture war debates regarding the proper academic mission of American higher education. I clearly have views on this
matter and these views inform much of what I have to say, but my primary
concern is to clarify fiscal and managerial issues that cut across the culture
war debate. Moreover, I would suggest that most of these culture war
debates cannot be meaningfully resolved without confronting their fiscal
implications. Again I have included references to this issue in notes.

The heated debate that presently revolves around the cost of higher education covers a number of different, often confused issues. One clearly deals
with the issue of cost. Another related but quite distinct issue deals with the
question of what we, as individuals and as a society, are willing to pay for
such an education. It is one thing to determine what a second home in the
country might cost and quite another to decide what one is willing to pay for
such a home. A third issue deals with the question of who should absorb this
cost: students, parents, the academic institutions, taxpayers, or some combination of all?

Clearly the issues are interrelated. If we have allocated an amount for an
item that is less then the item costs, we must decide either to forgo it, spend
more, or find some way to reconfigure the item so it costs less. If we elect to
spend more, there is a good chance that we will have less for other things.
Before we can determine if resources need to be reallocated, however, the
initial costs must be specified. This study will focus on what the basic costs
of American higher education presently are, what they buy, and who is paying for what.

Given that so much misinformation exists around these issues, I have also
elected to explain why there is a tendency to misread and misinterpret the
fiscal landscape of higher education. This part of my analysis has two related
but distinct purposes. In explaining why so much misinformation flourishes,
I hope to persuade the reader to accept what I expect will be some surprising and somewhat troubling facts. I also want to show how this misinformation has fostered actions that have served to aggravate rather than rectify an
already difficult situation. A central thesis of this study is that many, if not
most, proclaimed attempts to improve the financial state of American higher
education, which generally take the form of imposing managerial and fiscal
structures drawn from the corporate world, end up increasing costs and
decreasing educational productivity. Moreover, they tend to have other significant corollary negative educational effects by lowering academic morale
and undermining efficient decision making.

Having described the false diagnoses and faulty cures in the first two sections of this book, I attempt, in the third section, to suggest directions that we might take in an attempt to both conserve financial resources and enhance the quality of American higher education. The central task required here is to convince faculties that it is in their interest to accept fiscal responsibility for their own actions and institutions. I must admit that after thirty-five years in academic life dealing with fellow faculty, administrators, parents, and legislators, I am not that optimistic. The forces working against American higher education are many and deep-rooted. They are not easily resolved by any combination of organizational and fiscal adaptive procedures. On the other hand, there is evidence that some innovations not only can save money but also enhance the educational experience. More expensive doesn't necessarily mean better when it comes to higher education.

In making this point, I review in Part III some of the most promising initiatives that I encountered in recent years. Many of these initiatives require courage and willingness on the part of everyone involved to do things a little differently than they have become accustomed. If American higher education is to maintain the laudable international status that it has attained, however, considerable change will be necessary. The first step required is that we accept the fiscal reality we face. The second is to recognize that the management solutions being offered by most have and will only make things worse. The third step requires identifying those practices that appear to work and discovering ways in which they can be implemented in expanded ways.

This book is a product of two long-term interests that have defined my professional life. The first, a thirty-five-year commitment to higher education that has embraced not only an academic career as a teacher, scholar, and faculty member, but also over twelve years as an academic administrator, including five as a dean of faculty. I have also been an active fund-raiser for thirty years and more recently have served intermittently as an academic consultant. The second major influence has been my research in economic sociology and, more specifically, thirty plus years studying economic markets of varying sorts. During this time I have benefited from the advice and counsel of too many colleagues, friends, and acquaintances to name; however, a significant number must be noted.

I would like to begin by noting two groups: my own teachers and professors who instilled in me many years ago a deep appreciation for American higher education and my many students who have forged this appreciation into a commitment. I am also thankful to my many sociological colleagues with whom I have discussed various aspects of this study over the years. I am particularly indebted to my colleagues at Queens College and the Graduate Center, especially from those in the Sociology Department for their contributions to this project during the last thirty-five years. I am especially indebted to Andy Beveridge, Cynthia Epstein, Ray Franklin, Joanne Miller, Fred Purnell, Dean Savage, and the entire Monday lunch group for not only sharing their experiences with me but also for sharing their commitment to public higher education.

Over the years, this project has received, directly and indirectly, significant financial and psychological institutional support not only from Queens College, but also from the Ford Foundation; AAC&U; the Department of Education FIPSE program; and my alma mater, Wesleyan University.

I am particularly grateful to Edgar Beckham, Doug Bennet, Charles Karelis, Shirley Strum Kenny, Carol Schneider, and Allan Lee Sessoms. I also want to thank Dick Huddleston, Peter Manicas, Charles Olton, and David Potts, all of whom in sundry ways have been part of this process over many years. For research assistance, I am also in debt to Dana Lockwood and Pinh Boc.

Lengthy projects such as this extract a particularly high toll on the family of the author. They are forced to live through the various iterations, starts and stops, and ups and downs that any long-term project is bound to generate. For both their patience and intellectual input, I would like to thank my children, Abigail and Jonathan, and most especially my wife, Rita. I would also like to thank the Rowman & Littlefield team, without whom I doubt that I would have ever brought this project to fruition: Jill Rothenberg, who pushed me to find my particular voice; the production team of Patricia Waldygo and Janice Braunstein; and Dean Birkenkamp, who managed to keep a firm but open hand on the operation from beginning to end.

Part I

The Pitfalls of False Economic Diagnoses

1

~

Runaway Costs

Allegations and Reality

"How the heck do you academics manage to get away with it? You seem to be able to charge anything you want, do what you want, and get away with it. In my business, I'd never be able to do what you do."

How many times in recent years have I heard this refrain from both friends and strangers? More than I'd like to remember. Having spent the last thirty-five years in academia as a faculty member and in a range of administrative positions, including departmental chair, dean, and special assistant to the president, I guess I am a legitimate target. Nevertheless, I still get annoyed, especially when the question is followed up with an attack on lazy faculty members or inefficient administrators. What really frustrates me, however, is the unspoken assumption underlying these comments that higher education is clearly overpriced and that practically anyone, especially any businessperson or corporate manager, could and would be significantly more efficient and economical.

One of the major themes of this book is that they couldn't and wouldn't. They couldn't and wouldn't because most academic institutions have historically been run in a highly efficient, if organizationally unorthodox, manner. Such an assertion admittedly seems to contradict what most Americans accept as incontrovertible fact—namely, that the cost of higher education has skyrocketed out of proportion to the cost increases of nearly everything else.[1] No one denies, for example, that tuition costs of $1,000 a year in the late 1950s and early 1960s at many of the more expensive private colleges and universities rose to over $20,000 by the mid-1990s.[2] This is an inflation rate of approximately 2000 percent. Though the tuition costs at many other institutions, including most public institutions, have not reached this level, the proportional increase has often been larger.[3] Overall inflation for the same period was less than half this rate.[4]

3

When the price of anything increases at double the rate of inflation, especially when inflation itself has been pretty robust, questions are bound to be asked. Moreover, when the price reaches levels that cause many people to believe that they can no longer afford the item, this questioning is likely to be spiced with anger. The figures just presented, however, are highly misleading because they confuse the real cost of higher education with the *sticker* price—namely, tuition. They are seldom the same. Tuition normally covers only a portion of the total cost.

Given the high cost of tuition, this may not be an auspicious place to begin for someone claiming that the costs of higher education have not been mismanaged. It is an important distinction to make, however, since the price of tuition has generally risen much more sharply in recent years than the overall cost of higher education. Put quite simply, a much greater percentage of the overall cost is now allocated to tuition than was the case forty years ago. The proportion of the overall cost allocated to tuition—as well as the dollar amount for both overall cost and tuition cost—varies considerably from institution to institution. Moreover, it is often very difficult to determine what these figures are because different institutions use very different accounting methods and, depending upon the institution, these costs cover a wide range of activities.[5] Whatever these complications, however, even a superficial analysis reveals that tuition seldom covers more than 80 percent and often as little as 20 percent of the total cost of higher education. Where tuition costs normally run between $2,500 to $25,000 per year, total costs more commonly run from between $9,000 to over $40,000 per year.[6] Even at these levels, it must be noted that these costs do not include such things as room and board, books, laundry, and so forth.

It isn't surprising, given that many people don't earn $40,000 a year, that these figures cause eyebrows to rise. Thirty-five years ago, you could buy a substantial house for this amount of money in an expensive neighborhood; you can still buy a reasonable house for this amount of money in many places. How is it possible, people ask, for these institutions to justify such costs? How can they charge $25,000 a year, or even $18,000 a year, for tuition or justify annual costs of nearly $40,000? How can we expect states to spend hundreds of millions of dollars each year to support public higher education when there are so many other social needs? When it comes to most public institutions, where tuition tends to be significantly lower, critical attention is commonly focused on total budgets and overall tax liability generated by increased costs.

The answer to these questions is quite simple. Costs are so high because this is what it takes to provide the type of education expected. Higher education is a highly labor-intensive commodity, requiring an expensive infrastructure. Moreover, these labor costs have risen more rapidly than have most other costs, giving higher education a higher rate of inflation than most other sectors.[7] It is, as such, a very, very expensive good. First, it requires a highly and, consequently, expensively trained labor force—its faculty. Depending on the discipline and specialty, it normally takes anywhere from four to ten years of postgraduate study to earn the required doctorate degree. Moreover, a quality education demands that the ratio of faculty to students be maintained at a sufficiently high level to provide for personal attention. Colleges and universities must provide an extensive and expensive support structure. There is a need for teaching and laboratory assistants, clerical and secretarial staff, as well as maintenance personnel. There is also normally a need to maintain a large physical plant and to provide necessary supplies and equipment. All of these things cost money.

The criticism of higher education, however, clearly involves more than its high price. A high price, in and of itself, doesn't always create protest. At times, in fact, a high price conveys a sense of quality and is actually coveted. There is even strong evidence of this phenomenon in higher education, where the most expensive elite schools seem to receive less flak for their high tuition costs than do less expensive institutions.[8] It is not the high cost, per se, that seems to disturb people, as much as it is the belief, feeling—call it what you will—that the high price is somehow illegitimate. As noted earlier, there seems to be a pervasive assumption that nearly anyone else could do it more cheaply.

We will have an opportunity later to examine some of these assumptions, but comparative data would indicate that these costs are the norm for similar types of educational enterprises. Put simply, all forms of higher education appear to be inherently expensive commodities, no matter who is in charge. Comparing how much similar educational commodities cost in other settings reveals this.[9]

Colleges and universities are not the only institutions that are engaged in providing higher, or further, education. Nearly every company and organization in the country provides some sort of training and education to its employees, especially to its new recruits. This training covers the full gamut from what might be considered remedial learning and lower-level technical skills to the most sophisticated technical and theoretical instruction.

One organization that covers the whole gamut is the United States military, which provides a range of different training and educational programs—from basic training programs in the various services to advanced technical and officer-training programs. Whereas most colleges and universities structure their offerings in terms of eight sixteen-week semesters,[10] or the equivalent, given over a four-year period, the military concentrates on what are generally called basic training modules that run from eight to eleven weeks, depending upon the particular branch of the service. The military also supports a rich array of more advanced technical programs and officer-training programs, as well as a number of renowned military academies, including

West Point, Annapolis, and the Air Force Academy. These academies are structured similarly to most nonmilitary colleges.

How do the costs of these programs compare to the costs of our private and public colleges and universities?[11] Here we run into the problem of not only trying to compare different types of training over different lengths of time, but, perhaps more troubling, very different and often incomplete accounting reports. Nevertheless, it is possible to make some general comparisons. What we find is that the military doesn't seem to do any better, if as well, than typical institutions of higher education.

Even if we take for our comparison the high-end cost figure of $40,000 per year for the most expensive colleges and universities, and the least expensive military training, which is the Army's eight-week basic training program, we discover that our institutions of higher education come off quite well by comparison. Assuming an average academic year of two sixteen-week semesters, for a total of thirty-two weeks of education per year, the weekly cost at even the more expensive elite liberal education colleges averages approximately $1,250. By using figures for the overall costs of different programs divided by the number of individuals run through these different military programs, it is possible to generate rough cost figures for these various military training and educational programs. Based on these figures, the cost of an eight-week basic training course in the United States Army in 1996 and 1997 was somewhere between $21,000 and $22,000 per person. This works out to almost $3,000 per week per person, which is nearly two-and-a-half times the rate of most Ivy League colleges.

What is somewhat more disconcerting is the fact that the Army's basic training program is the cheapest program run by the U.S. military establishment. The Navy's basic training program for the same two-year period costs between $29,600 and $36,000 per person, for a program that runs seven weeks. This works out to between $4,000 and $5,000 per person per week. The basic training program for the Marine Corps during the same two-year period costs significantly in excess of $50,000 per recruit for an eleven-week program. This also works out to approximately $5,000 per week. The Air Force's basic training program, which does not include flight training, for these same two years averages slightly less than $40,000 per recruit for a six-week program, which comes out to approximately $6,500 per person per week.

Technical training costs considerably more than basic training. Again, the Army tends to be the least expensive, but even in the Army technical training costs more than the most expensive university. While the Army is able to run its technical skill courses for approximately $33,000 per student, the Air Force requires on average $44,000, the Navy spends $60,000, and the Marine Corps comes out on top with $75,000 per student. While it is nearly impossible to do a rigorous weekly breakdown of these figures, it appears that the weekly costs of technical training across the military branches are 10 to 25 percent more than each branch's weekly cost of basic training.

The cost of flight training, as might be expected, dwarfs all of these figures. The annual cost per participant is pretty much the same across the various services, running in excess of $400,000 per participant in 1996, but dropping back to a real bargain price of approximately $360,000 per participant in 1997. Fortunately, the Marine Corps, which seems to run the most expensive programs, doesn't operate its own flight-training program. Even when the cost of flight training is subtracted, the average overall weekly cost of military training exceeds $5,000 a week. In comparison, the $1,300 to $1,400 weekly expenditures of Harvard, let alone the $400 to $600 expenditures of most state universities, would seem to be a bargain.[12]

It might be argued that all of the various military programs discussed here are integral parts of the military services taken as a whole. Given the financial pressure and criticism to which the military is constantly subject, the top brass may have created a system in which sizable chunks of general overhead costs are attributed to training activities because it is easier to defend such training activities. Nobody wants to be responsible for providing insufficient training that results in unnecessary deaths. As such, it could be argued that a better comparison would be with the various military academies that function more strictly as colleges.

While such comparisons probably are more appropriate, the costs of these academies are actually higher. Various estimates have been made of the overall cost to put a person through four years of a military academy. The figures reported in the Department of Education's postsecondary data system for 1991 through 1995 average approximately $65,000 per student annually. These figures, however, don't include major costs that are absorbed into the various military budgets. The true costs for four years have been claimed to fluctuate around $1,000,000; this works out to an annual cost of $250,000.[13] My own best estimate is that when all personnel and plant costs, student stipends and benefits, and special equipment expenses are included, the true cost averages around half a million dollars per student, which works out to $125,000 per year. The fact that this figure is about double the publicly acknowledged amount and half of what some critics claim makes me believe that it is probably pretty close to the right figure. Even $125,000 a year is qualitatively different than $40,000. For that matter, so is $75,000, which is what the 1995 data works out to for West Point.

The military, of course, has had its own problems regarding its reputation for efficient management. Who can forget the stories of $500 wrenches and $1,000 toilet seats? The fact that the military spends more than nonmilitary colleges and universities spend doesn't exactly resolve the issue. Rather than implying that other institutions of higher education are actually quite frugal, these figures, it could easily be argued, only show that our institutions of higher education are not alone in being profligate. The fact is, however, not only do our institutions of higher education and the military find education to be expensive. Higher education proves to be expensive no matter who is in charge—even when those providing it are our most hardheaded business organizations.

Nearly every major corporation in America runs some sort of training program; significant portions of these programs are similar in form and content to courses offered by institutions of higher education.[14] Some of these programs are in house while others are subcontracted out, often to any of a number of business schools. What is important to note is that even when these programs are subcontracted out, the corporations maintain fairly close fiscal control over the programs. They may not engage in the actual budgeting of the programs, but they require fairly detailed accounting reports and generally negotiate with a number of different institutions before entering into a contract. Clearly, price is not the only item that concerns them, but it is seldom, if ever, ignored. So what do we find when these masters of industry are in charge? Pretty much the same thing that we found when the generals and admirals were in charge.

Let's begin with the programs subcontracted to business schools because these figures are more easily accessed and interpreted.[15]

Close to 40 different educational institutions offer on a regular basis over 130 different types of management training courses for American and foreign corporations. Of these courses, all but 12 or so are offered under the sponsorship of some college or university, generally their business school. These programs run from one week to almost a full year. Most of these programs focus on finance, marketing, operations, technical issues, business strategy, leadership, and organizational behavior and run for only one to two weeks. Courses in public affairs and government, human resource development, and general humanities normally also run for one to two weeks. Approximately half of the sixty general management programs run for three to six weeks, with approximately a half-dozen running from seven to twelve weeks and four lasting forty to fifty weeks. Except for one technical program, these are the only programs that run for approximately one year. The cost of some of these programs, especially the one- to two-week programs, includes room and board.

How do the costs of these programs compare with the normal programs offered by these educational institutions? Not unexpectedly, they vary. The only consistent thing is that even the least expensive programs cost more than the $1,250 a week of the most expensive private colleges. With the exception of one very expensive three-week program run by the Wharton School of the University of Pennsylvania, which is priced at $12,000 per week, the cost of nearly all of these programs, once adjustments are made for room and board, is $2,000 to $4,000 per week. Interestingly, the average cost of approximately $3,000 per week is not that different from the cost of training in the Army.

What about in-house programs? Here, we have a real difficulty in obtaining honest cost figures—we must rely on figures that are self-disclosed by the various corporate entities—and then we have the added problem of attempting to make these figures comparable. I have spent a good deal of time attempting to get these figures from a few corporations that run well-publicized and formal in-house training programs. By and large, I have found that these companies really don't have the figures themselves, since it is very difficult to identify, isolate, and allocate all of the true costs of such programs.[16] What does seem fairly clear, however, is that in nearly all cases, the in-house costs are actually higher than costs for subcontracting similar training. As one senior management person said in response to my question, "Why do you think we are willing to spend the significant sums we are spending to send our people to Wharton, Stanford, and Harvard? We do it because it is cheaper."

The World Bank, for example, computed its in-house educational budget for 1997 at slightly more than $36,000,000. From the annual World Bank report,[17] it is impossible to break this figure down in terms of the various educational programs, but rough approximations can be made. What we find is that these programs cost minimally over $3,000 per participant per week to nearly $10,000 per participant per week.[18]

The problem here, of course, might be that these corporations simply have too much money to throw around. They know how to be efficient and could be if they so desired, but for various reasons they like to go first class when it comes to corporate training. While there probably is some truth to such criticisms, the fact is, even the poorest buyers of education seem unable to keep costs down. Here I refer not to those engaged in purchasing higher education but to those purchasing apparently less expensive elementary and secondary education. In this context, it is worth noting that in many of our more wealthy suburbs, the cost of K–12 education is in excess of $15,000 per student per year, with K–12 education in some communities costing over $20,000 per student.[19] Even in less affluent communities, fewer and fewer communities are managing on less than $10,000 per student. In short, by all comparisons it seems that education is simply a very expensive commodity.

It might still be argued that just because everyone is overpaying, this doesn't prove anything. The problem may be that everyone—colleges and universities, the military, corporations, and our local school boards—is grossly inefficient. This is, in fact, what some critics seem to be saying. The problem may stem from a lack of market controls due to the fact that the providers—that is, the educators, like "professionals" in any market situation—have an unfair advantage when it comes to setting prices. Like lawyers, doctors, and other knowledge professionals, academic administrators and professors may be able to control their market price and charge what they like. It could be argued that the consistency we find in the previous figures shows that not only is everyone getting ripped off, but there is also a massive conspiracy behind the rip-off.

Fortunately, there is another way to unpack the figures with which we have been playing. We can engage in a little cost analysis. The idea here is to switch our focus from what education presently costs to the question of what it should cost, or at least what it might cost given various assumptions.

Given the labor-intensive nature of higher education noted earlier, it makes sense to begin with labor costs.[20] This requires determining the quantity of different types of labor required and the cost of this labor. These figures vary considerably from institution to institution and depend on a wide range of factors, including faculty salaries, faculty-to-student ratios, support staff, and other such categories. Moreover, all of these factors can legitimately be debated. To move our discussion forward, I will simply proceed, drawing upon my own thirty-five-plus years as both a college teacher and an administrator. I will introduce various conversion ratios later to cover other conditions and assumptions.

One of the first factors that needs to be determined in computing the cost of education is the appropriate student–faculty ratio. This ratio is determined by a wide range of considerations, including the number of courses students take, the number of courses professors teach, and the ratio among different types of classes offered. One factor that is central, however, is the actual number of students a professor teaches in a given class. Here again, there tends to be a wide range, with most colleges offering both small seminars that may have less than ten students and large lecture courses with over one hundred students. Moreover, these practices vary considerably from college to college.

There does tend to be some uniformity, however, in the expected range of class sizes in most liberal education colleges, especially the more highly regarded "elite" ones. In these institutions, seminars generally run from six to the high teens and average around ten students. Most other classes have, at minimum, twenty students and can run into the hundreds. The overall average tends to be in the mid-thirties. Put together, this commonly generates an average class size of approximately twenty. Admittedly, there are colleges where the average class size is less and considerably more schools where the average class size is more than double this figure. To keep things relatively simple and because we are interested in setting an upper limit, however, it makes sense to begin with this twenty-to-one ratio.

A twenty-to-one student-to-faculty classroom ratio, however, does not normally convert into an overall twenty-to-one student-to-faculty ratio. Faculty members, especially at the more prestigious colleges and universities, are expected to do more than teach their classes. They are expected to pursue their own research agenda and to publish the results of this research in scholarly publications. This is the basis of the famous, or infamous, adage "publish or perish." In addition, faculty members have various advisement and administrative activities such as maintaining attendance rosters, grade records, and so on. Each institution has its own particular system of accounting for these various activities in determining faculty members' teaching responsibilities, but it is possible to follow some general guidelines. The object of these guidelines is to generate a full, but reasonable, workload.

For students, such a workload usually entails taking four or five courses per semester. This requires that they normally spend between twelve to sixteen hours in class each week. In addition, they are expected to match this classroom time with, at minimum, double the number of hours studying and/or in laboratories. This comes to thirty-six to forty-eight hours on average per week, with some students managing to get by with as few as twenty-five hours a week while others put in workweeks in excess of sixty hours.

Faculty members, in addition to the hours they spend in the classroom, require time to prepare lectures and presentations; to grade homework assignments, papers, and exams; and to maintain office hours and attend student conferences. Here again, the nature of the mix and the amount of time actually required vary from campus to campus. Generally, three hours for these duties outside the classroom are required for every hour in the classroom.[21] In addition, faculty members need time to pursue their own research. Consequently, while students are expected to put in a full week on their classroom work, most faculty members are expected to divide their time between teaching and research. In some cases a fifty-fifty split is the norm. In others cases, a sixty-forty or even three-to-one mix is the norm. Whereas students generally take between four and five classes per semester, professors in most colleges teach between two and four courses per semester, with the lower teaching loads more common in the more prestigious and more research-oriented institutions.

Despite significant differences in professors' classroom responsibilities from one institution to another, the actual total time consumed by, with, and for students tends to even out. In the more prestigious liberal education colleges, where professors may normally spend only six hours a week teaching two classes to a comparatively small number of students, they are also likely to meet with students six to ten hours per week. Similarly, professors in major research institutions who spend relatively few hours in class normally devote many hours to conferences with graduate students. In contrast, in those institutions where faculty members may be required to teach classes nine hours per week with twice the number of students, the time demands put upon them to meet with students may be only a few hours per week. The reason for this is that many more of their students are likely to have part-time, or even-full time, jobs that dramatically cut down on the time these students have for their studies. Moreover, these institutions are often commuter colleges where it is more difficult to meet with faculty outside of the classroom. The key issue, in short, really isn't how many hours a week a faculty member spends in class, but rather how many hours a week he or she spends in teaching. In institutions that expect faculty to be engaged in research, most faculty members are expected to spend between 50 and 60 percent of their time on teaching.

It should be noted, however, that this doesn't leave the rest of the time free for research. In addition to their teaching and student obligations, faculty members have various departmental and college administrative responsibilities. When the ten to fifteen hours a week required to carry on even a minimal research agenda are added to the previously mentioned workload, few faculty members end up with a workweek of less than forty hours. For those pursuing research activities for twenty-plus hours a week, fifty- to sixty-hour weeks are the norm.[22]

Here it should be stressed that with the exception of senior tenured professors, none of this can be considered voluntary activity on the part of the faculty. There is a good deal of talk and criticism about academic tenure and research, much of it implying that these practices are controlled by the faculty. This is not the case. Tenure might be a desirable perquisite once it is obtained, but junior faculty members don't have any choice in the matter. You either earn tenure or you leave. The issue of promotion isn't quite as stark. Once tenured, you can normally preserve your job even if you are not promoted, but there are significant financial and personal costs entailed in being passed over for promotion year after year. In short, research time isn't your own time. It is institutional time, as much as is the time you spend in the classroom or correcting exams. We will return to this issue in the next chapter. Again as before, there are differences from institution to institution, with some institutions placing significantly fewer research demands upon the faculty. Since we will be able to correct our ratios later for these situations, they need not concern us here.

Whatever the differences from institution to institution, the bottom line implication of faculty members' additional commitments is that classroom ratios don't convert exactly into faculty–student ratios. While the actual numbers vary, in most cases the final conversion factor is approximately two to one. To be more specific, in most elitist schools, be they small colleges or research institutions, where students generally take four courses per semester, faculty members teach two courses. In the more numerous comprehensive four-year institutions, where students commonly take five courses per semester, faculty members might teach three courses per semester, with an occasional course off for extra institutional obligations. For the most part, therefore, a two-to-one ratio tends to hold, which means that if we start with an average class size of twenty students per faculty member, we have moved to a ten-to-one overall faculty-to-student ratio. Unfortunately, we aren't done yet with this downward correction.

Not all faculty members are available to teach. While higher education does employ some full-time administrators, faculty members occupy many administrative jobs, such as chairing departments for which they normally receive reduced teaching loads. At the departmental level, such administrative released time generally does not exceed 10 to 15 percent of teaching time. From an administrative/organizational perspective this is quite efficient. There are also, of course, other nondepartmental administrative duties occupied by faculty appointments such as academic deans, which increase these ratios. In addition, a percentage of faculty is always unavailable to teach during a given semester because of sabbatical leaves. Depending upon the institution, this can generate an additional loss of available faculty of 5 to 15 percent.[23] When faculty availability is adjusted for administrative and leave losses, our student-to-faculty ratio of ten to one is reduced to seven to one.[24] I should stress that we are admittedly modeling the most expensive and prestigious institutions.

It is at this point that we need to put dollar figures on our calculations. How much should we be willing to pay the faculty? Obviously, we are not going to pay them all the same. Some are just starting out, with few credentials, while others have years of experience, lengthy publication lists, highly funded grants, and international reputations. Even the most junior member of the faculty, however, has completed on average eight years of postgraduate study and has a doctorate. People with commensurate credentials in law, business, or medicine are likely to be paid in excess of forty dollars an hour just out of graduate school, with the more senior people earning three to five times as much. But college faculties are, after all, still just teachers. On the other hand, we are talking about the supposedly best faculty at our most prestigious colleges and universities. In light of this, I would suggest that an average hourly rate of thirty dollars, which works out to an annual average salary of $60,000, is as low as we should go. While this is higher than the national average, I think it must be agreed that it is a modest salary, given that it is presented as an average salary for individuals who have completed anywhere from three to ten years of postgraduate study, written a thesis, and spent many years in near poverty as graduate students. It is also probably a fair estimate of the average pay for the more highly paid senior faculty members at one of our more prestigious institutions.

Now $60,000 to cover seven students doesn't seem to add up to the $40,000 per student cost we started with. Unfortunately, the $60,000 is still just the beginning. The hard facts are that it takes a lot more than a faculty, even with chairs and a few deans thrown in, to run a college. A faculty requires a secretarial and clerical support staff. Moreover, a college needs people to run its admission and financial aid offices. People are needed to staff the library, the computer and science labs, and the registrar's and bursar's offices. Once these people have been paid, there is also the cost of their fringe benefits. In addition to these costs, a physical plant must be maintained and run, which requires not only a staff but also money for such things as oil, electricity, supplies, and so on. Again, the actual figures vary from campus to campus, but certain minimum needs can be calculated.

In many (more well-endowed) institutions, the general operating rule is that faculty salaries constitute at most 50 percent of overall salaries. This ratio is necessary if the institution is also to provide a secretary or clerical support person for every four faculty members, another support staff person for every three faculty members on average to run the various nonteaching clerical and administrative departments, another staff person for every three faculty members for maintenance, and finally a senior administrative person for every twenty-five faculty members. In the less highly endowed institutions, the ratio of faculty salaries to nonfaculty costs is normally higher, with faculty accounting for up to 65 percent of salaries. Given that we are working with the student cost of $40,000 attributed to the richest institutions, I will go with the fifty-fifty split for now. This doubles our costs, from $60,000 to $120,000.

Even $120,000 is less than half of the $280,000 figure that our seven-to-one ratio and $40,000 annual cost would dictate, but all costs haven't yet been included. One of these is fringe benefits. They include everything from the 7 percent FICA charge to retirement and health benefits that have historically run on the high side in universities and colleges, in part to offset what have been traditionally lower salaries. The percentage cost of such a fringe package varies from a low of 20 percent to over 30 percent. If we elect to go with an overall fringe benefits package costing 30 percent, our salary costs are increased from $120,000 to $160,000.[25] This still does not reach $280,000, but we haven't yet included one penny for supplies, buildings, repairs, and so on. Here again, the wealthier institutions generally commit approximately 50 percent of their operating costs to their physical plant and supplies. Using this 50-percent figure, our $160,000 expense budget jumps to $320,000, which is actually $40,000 more than the $280,000 that we computed, based on the top cost of $40,000 per student.[26] At $320,000 the cost per student is actually over $45,000. And we haven't built in any costs for special items such as museums, athletics, and other extracurricular activities commonly offered, which require institutional subsidies.

The various calculations presented here can be put into a fairly simple formula: (AFC + FB) ÷ (ACS × TSCR × FA × FSR) ÷ PCTC = ECS. In English, it reads as follows: Average Faculty Compensation (AFC) plus Fringe Benefits (FB), divided by Average Class Size (ACS), adjusted for the ratio of classes taught by a teacher to classes taken by a student (TSCR = Teacher-to-Student

Class Ratios), then adjusted for the percentage of faculty on salary available to teach (FA = Faculty Availability), and further adjusted for the percentage of faculty cost to total staff costs (FSR = Faculty-to-Staff Ratio). This figure is then adjusted by the percentage of total personnel costs to total costs, including physical plant, supplies, and so on (PCTC = Personnel Costs to Total Cost). The resulting figure equals the educational cost per student (ECS). With the figures used here, the formula would read as follows: ($60,000 + $20,000) ÷ (20 × .5 × .7 × .5) ÷ .50 = $45,714.28.

We could clearly make adjustments to these ratios. We could increase our average class size by 50 percent. This would increase our classroom ratio from twenty-to-one to thirty-to-one. We could also increase the average number of classes taught by the faculty by a third. This would convert our .5 ratio into a .67 ratio. Similarly, we could cut released time for leaves and administration by a third. This would increase the percentage of available teaching time to 80 percent (.8). We could similarly assume less support staff and increase our ratio of faculty costs to total staff costs from 50 percent (.5) to 65 percent (.65). Finally, we could cut back on the cost of supplies and investment in the physical plant, allowing us to spend 60 percent on salaries. With all of these quite dramatic changes, holding our salary and fringe package costs the same, the formula would read as follows: ($60,000 + $20,000) ÷ (30 × .65 × .8 × .65) ÷ .60 = $12,380.07, which approximates fairly well what most underfunded state systems cost at present.

Before anyone gets too excited by these cost reductions, I should point out that they represent serious staff and facility reductions that impact negatively on the educational process. The educational experience that can be bought for $12,000 per student per year isn't the educational experience most people have in mind when they think of a traditional liberal arts and sciences college education. A $12,000 per student per year, education entails few, if any, small classes and little faculty-to-student interaction. Most laboratories are likely to be poorly supplied, the library will have relatively few scientific journals and current publications, and the buildings and grounds are likely to be in need of repair. In short, it won't be the charming campus of well-kept buildings and playing fields, available faculty members, and opportunities for individual pursuit of knowledge that we often envisage when we think of a college education. This is a college with a student-to-faculty ratio of approximately twenty-five to one with a "bare bones" campus. At this college an undersubscribed course—that is, a course with less than ten or maybe even fifteen students—will be canceled even if this means that some students will not be able to graduate within four years. To look at it from the other side, the movie version of the elite college with intense student-to-faculty interactions; lovely dorms; athletic facilities for football, soccer, baseball, and fencing; and art collections would find it difficult to survive today even on the $45,714.28 per student budget computed earlier.

While our formula can be adjusted to reduce costs, it can also be used to explain how easily costs can increase. It doesn't require much juggling to understand how the various military academies could spend annually $65,000 or even $150,000 per student.[27] To begin with, the staff-to-student ratios tend to be much lower than those of even the most well-endowed private college. The cost ratios of support staff to instructors as well as of physical plant and supplies to personnel are also significantly more expensive. On top of these costs, military cadets receive salaries while attending the military academy. When these differences are plugged into our formula, it isn't that difficult to get to $65,000, $125,000, or even $250,000.[28]

So what are we to make of these figures? They certainly haven't made higher education any cheaper. What I hope they have done is reveal that educational costs rest on a range of factors and that there is nothing inherently illegitimate about these high costs. It should also be noted that there isn't any evidence that the price of education has risen in an outrageous or crazy manner. Admittedly, $12,000—not to mention $45,000 and $125,000—is a lot of money, but in 1960 terms, this converts to approximately $1,000, $4,000, and $12,000, which is what a similar education cost then. (We will take a closer look at this issue shortly.) The reality is that the product, higher education, is inherently expensive. If anything, our institutions of higher education seem to be constraining costs as well as might be expected. They are certainly doing as well as the military and private corporations. More important, a breakdown of their costs seems quite reasonable. This doesn't preclude our rethinking whether we can afford such a product or whether we really need such an expensive product. In fact, as we will shortly see, these are questions that require our attention. The previous analysis, however, would seem to indicate that given the product we have and the product we seem to want, the price seems to be sound. There are good reasons to believe, in fact, that we might actually be underbudgeted in many if not most situations.[29] By way of contrast, compared to the $30,000 to $40,000 spent to support a person in prison, the money spent on education is worthwhile.

Assuming that our comparisons and calculations are correct, the next question that arises is why nearly everyone should have the opinion that the cost of higher education has increased in an irresponsible manner. What we will discover is that a whole range of psychological factors serve to reinforce this misperception.

2

~

Why Education
Seems So Expensive

If the cost of American higher education is as legitimate as the first chapter claims, why do so many people think the cost is outrageous? A number of factors have contributed to this misperception, but probably the most important factor has been inflation or, more correctly, long-term inflation. As noted in chapter 1, the cost of nearly everything has gone up dramatically during the last thirty to forty years, due to steady and, at times, rampant inflation. There has, in fact, been a full eightfold increase in costs from 1957 to 1997, based on the government's Composite Commodity Price Index. But why should the cost of higher education draw more criticism than almost everything else? The reason is quite simple. Higher education is not a product that most people buy on a regular basis. Whereas some products are bought weekly, several decades normally intercede between purchases of higher education. This contributes significantly to what might be called "sticker shock."

While prices have increased eightfold during the last forty years, for example, the average annual rate has been qualitatively less. Since 1957, we have had only seven years (1974, 1975, 1976, 1977, 1979, 1980, and 1981) when inflation ran into double-digits.[30] In contrast, for nearly twice that number of years inflation has actually been under 5 percent per year. Here we have another example of the miracle of compounded rates. We normally only hear about the advantages of such compounding, such as the bank advertisement that $1,000, earning only 7.5 percent interest, will be worth approximately $10,000 in thirty years. The bad news is that a similar rate of inflation will generate a similar ten times inflation rate in thirty years. While such a tenfold increase is striking, it is not likely to be experienced as such on a daily or even yearly basis. This is evidenced by the fact that, with the exception of the years of double-digit inflation under Presidents Carter and Reagan, inflatio⸍

day-to-day basis hasn't been a major concern during the last thirty- to forty-year period. People don't like paying more for anything, but when the increases come gradually, day by day, they seem to take them in stride.

Such acceptance, however, doesn't apply to items that we seldom buy. This is perfectly understandable when we realize that while the cost increase of an item we buy weekly is likely to be almost imperceptible, the increase on an item bought every thirty years will be huge. More concretely, a 10-percent inflation rate works out to less than a .2 percent weekly rate. This converts into a two-cent increase on a $10 item. In contrast, a similar inflation rate of 10 percent works out to over a 60-percent increase in five years. The cost of a $10,000 automobile, for example, will increase to over $16,000 over a five-year period. Even if we reduce the inflation rate to 5 percent, the price of the $10,000 automobile will increase to approximately $12,250—a 22-percent increase. We tend to react more negatively to a 22-percent increase over five years than we do to a .2-percent weekly increase, even when the latter actually reflects a higher annual rate of inflation. This difference explains why "sticker shock" tends to be associated more with the purchase of big-ticket items that are bought only every few years, rather than with items bought daily or weekly.

This psychological mechanism is clearly at work when it comes to higher education. For most people first contemplating the sticker price of their children's college education, their last "purchase" occurred twenty to thirty years earlier when they were students. What they confront, consequently, isn't a .2-percent or even a 22-percent increase, but minimally a 1000-percent increase. This is the type of sticker shock that can throw otherwise rational people off stride.

But, it could be argued, as bad as a tenfold increase might be, the price of tuition, in many if not most instances, has actually gone up double this rate. This brings us to the second key factor at work in higher education. The price of tuition has also risen due to a major reallocation of the costs of higher education. More specifically, as indicated in chapter 1, during the last thirty or so years there has been a dramatic shift in the proportion of costs of higher education that have been allocated to tuition revenue. This represents perhaps the most significant and commonly ignored development in the funding of higher education. Put slightly differently, not only have costs gone up due to inflation and other factors, but students and their families are now being expected to absorb a larger percentage of these costs. An item we used to get at discount, we are now expected to pay full price, or nearly full price, for. What adds to the confusion is the fact that few people realize that higher education was historically sold at substantially less than cost.

The whole process reminds me of a "classic" confidence game that was commonly run on the game strips of the old traveling carnival shows. The basic idea behind the game is quite simple. Get the player to accept a false sense of what a game of chance costs by allowing him to win. Then increase the stakes of the game and stop allowing him to win. In short, play fairly. When the player begins to lose, he becomes confused as a result of his flawed understanding of the game, which was based on his earlier winning experience. He will often continue to play and lose money as he tries to figure out what is going on. Most players assume that the game operator is *now* cheating, when in reality he was cheating earlier when they were winning.

Setting up false expectations is a time-tested technique for getting people to focus on the wrong issue. In the case of the confidence game just noted, this technique is deliberately utilized. In other situations, false expectations may be more the result of unintended, or at least unplanned, actions. The latter situation seems to be the case with higher education. Whether planned or not, the negative implications due to misunderstanding and confusion can be just as costly.

As in the confidence game, higher education has given rise to false expectations by its past practices of giving something away for free or, more correctly, at a significant discount. I refer here to the fact that tuition, both historically and presently, covers only a percentage of the overall cost of education. More important, in the 1950s and 1960s tuition typically covered a much smaller proportion of educational costs than it typically does today. These facts are generally not recognized. As a result, what is commonly overlooked is that the great increase in tuition prices during the last thirty years has been due not only to a general increase in the cost of education but also to a greater reliance upon tuition revenues to cover this cost.

Here figures vary considerably from institution to institution, and the figures we have tend to be somewhat out of date. In addition, there are various reasons to question some of the figures reported. Nevertheless, even the figures that we have reveal the general trend toward increased reliance on tuition, if not the full extent of this change. Figures reported for 1960–1987, for example, indicate an overall increase in the reliance on tuition in public higher education to be from 20 to 24 percent.[31] In the last ten years, this trend has accelerated to the point that reliance on tuition is seldom less than 35 percent, and in many states it is now approximately 50 percent.[32] This works out on average to approximately a doubling of the reliance on tuition in public higher education since 1960. In some cases the percentage increases have been even greater. In the mid-'60s when I began teaching at Queens College of the City University of New York, there was no tuition. There were some student fees, but these fees covered considerably less than 10 percent of direct costs and less than 5 percent of total costs.[33] Today, the price of tuition equals approximately 40 percent of direct costs, and expectations are that this percentage will only increase in the years ahead. This works out to nearly a tenfold increase in the percentage of costs charged to students.

The analogous increase for private institutions overall was from a 64 percent reliance on tuition in 1960 to a 73 percent tuition reliance in 1987.[34] By 1997, the best estimate is that the overall reliance on tuition has grown to close to 80 percent. In many cases, however, especially among the better-endowed institutions, the increase has been considerably more since the starting point was considerably less than the average of 64 percent. In the case of certain elite private colleges such as Wesleyan University, which I attended in the late '50s, the reliance upon tuition was only 20 percent of total costs from the late '50s to the mid-'60s. By 1997 the overall figure had grown to approximately 80 percent. The beginning rate of 20 percent was admittedly considerably lower than that of most other institutions, but the reliance on tuition in 1960 for most highly endowed institutions was considerably lower than the average of 64 percent.[35]

Another way of understanding this same issue is to realize that in the private sector, reliance upon endowment dropped from approximately 20 percent in 1960 to approximately 10 percent by the mid-1990s. Given that most of this endowment was held by a small minority of the richest private institutions, the degree of change for these better-endowed colleges was much greater. A conservative estimate of the average drop in reliance on endowment for wealthier institutions would be from 20 to 50 percent. To offset this drop, these institutions were forced to double their reliance on tuition from approximately 40 percent in the early 1960s to around 80 percent today. In short, this is the same doubling that we saw with public institutions.

It is important to point out that the historical generosity of many of these private institutions was often due as much to their ignorance of the true cost of education as it was to a sense of charity. Many institutions of higher education, especially the private, older, and more established institutions, historically failed to calculate accurately their true costs. They failed, for example, to account for the depreciation costs of their physical plant or income potential of their real estate holdings. They often only recorded upkeep and maintenance expenses. Similarly, buildings and real estate were commonly carried on the books at a fraction of their true market value. There was a similar tendency to undervalue the actual worth of a wide range of donated services. In short, the historical failure to acknowledge the true expense of higher education in calculating tuition was due to negligence as often as munificence. Whatever the motivation, it seems as if tuition costs were commonly set, somewhat as an afterthought, at the level required to cover the institution's budgetary/cash shortfall.

The artificially low tuition rates of the past, coupled with the twofold increased reliance on tuition to cover costs, and the dramatic impact of even modest inflation over a thirty- to forty-year period explains why present tuition rates generate the shock that they do. The fact that the overall cost increase for higher education has actually been quite consistent with the overall inflation rate doesn't seem to matter. It seems to matter even less that given that higher education is a labor-intensive process, the actual cost increases have been quite reasonable.

This would seem to raise another question. If, as it has been argued, overall costs have increased at approximately the same rate as overall inflation, why has there been a need to allocate so much more of these costs to tuition?

There are a number of different reasons for this. Nearly all are related in some way or other to the overall growth of higher education. While most educational institutions experienced a growth in their endowments during this period, for example, few experienced sufficient growth to keep up with both the overall inflation rate and student growth. As a result, support per student from endowment decreased. An added difficulty experienced by many institutions was a growing tendency for donors to restrict their funds for specific pet projects. This further limited the amount of endowment subsidies available to support students. The same situation characterized funds available from most annual fund campaigns. The total amount of money raised and distributed increased overall, but the amounts raised per student, adjusted for inflation, decreased. There was similarly an increase in restricted giving, which left less unrestricted funds available to subsidize tuition.

For the public sector, the situation was, if anything, actually worse. While there has been significant growth in the number of students attending private colleges and universities during the last thirty years, the growth in those attending public institutions has been much greater. To fund this growth, there has been a dramatic increase in state and federal support of higher education. While this has resulted in increased tax support for higher education, year by year, the amount provided per student attending these public institutions, again adjusted for inflation, has actually decreased in recent years. As a result, these students have been forced to absorb more and more of their educational costs. Public support per student at Queens College, CUNY, for example, is today, adjusted for inflation, less than half of what it was when I started teaching there in 1965. While this is a fairly extreme case, given that Queens College charged no tuition in 1965, most other public institutions have experienced a similar decrease in public support *per student.*

While the overall growth in higher education has put strains on traditional nontuition funding sources, such growth has also served to reveal the hidden costs. As mentioned earlier, for many years, our higher education institutions had a tendency to underestimate significantly the real cost of the physical plant. As these educational institutions expanded, they discovered, often painfully, that it cost a great deal to augment and replace their physical plants. In many cases, the real—that is, market—costs of these assets were substantially if not completely ignored. It was not unusual, for example, for many institutions to make no accounting for the market value of these assets in determining the institution's overall annual expenses. That is, while they included such things as cost of repair and general upkeep in determining institutional costs, they commonly ignored the cost of capital that was invested in such buildings and real estate.

When such capital investments were recognized, they were often carried on the books at their original prices, which could easily be one-tenth or less of the true market value. The capital invested in a building constructed at the end of the nineteenth century for $10,000, for example, might be completely ignored or carried at its $10,000 cost, which, assuming a 6-percent cost of money, might then be shown as a $600 debit. The true market value of such a building, however, might well be several million dollars, with a true annual cost of hundreds of thousand of dollars. Such practices, in effect, constituted a significant subsidy to tuition.

This all changed dramatically with the arrival of thousands of new students who forced these institutions to undertake major physical plant expansions. As a consequence of such building programs, funds that previously were available to subsidize normal expenses were now required to support an expanding physical plant. In many cases, the increase in costs brought about by these new buildings and the purchase of additional real estate was exacerbated by the recognition that the existing plant had not been properly depreciated and expensed. The addition of a new, expanded physical plant often caused institutions to increase dramatically the value of their old plant. This, in turn, forced them to allocate increased reserve funds to offset depreciation of these buildings. These same pressures also commonly forced institutional administrations to redirect significant portions of funds raised through annual giving, previously available to subsidize normal operations, into buildings and equipment.

The fact that expenses for new buildings and increased maintenance costs, as well as more appropriate accounting procedures, have risen sharply and impacted negatively on institutional resources available to subsidize tuition should not obscure the fact that the real costs per student for physical plant and related items have, by and large, merely kept pace with inflation. The complaints accompanying these increases have been due primarily to a general failure to understand the process that caused this situation.

The costs of capital plants were not the only things that were commonly calculated at below market value forty years ago. Until the early 1960s, faculty salaries also tended to be "below" market value, if years of training and education were considered. Here again, the failure to keep abreast with changing market conditions was due to the underlying dynamics of a highly traditional system in which cost factors were commonly slighted. It wasn't until the growth pressures of the '60s, brought on to a large extent by concern with American higher education generated by the Russian Sputnik success, that faculty salaries became more competitive. In a relatively short period of time, the salaries of faculty nearly doubled in real terms as they increased at double the inflation rate.

Few people today remember just how low most academic salaries were. I am reminded of a story related to me in the mid-'60s when I was engaged in my first salary negotiation. It was June, quite late to make an appointment for the coming fall semester, but a senior faculty member had received a grant and had elected at the last moment to go on sabbatical. As a consequence, there weren't many job candidates available. I was available because I had a more than adequate fellowship and hadn't intended to teach in the fall. One of my professors, on hearing of the job, suggested that I go for the interview. He thought that it would not only be a good experience for me but would perhaps improve the chances for future, full-time positions at this college for doctoral graduates from our program.

The dean and I hit it off right away. I quickly decided that I would like the job and he seemed equally delighted to hire me. There was no problem in deciding when and what I would teach. The only issue that needed to be decided was what I would be paid. He offered $6,000 for the year, which was more than reasonable, but I requested $6,500. My request was based on the fact that I had a substantial tax-free fellowship and $6,000 just didn't seem to be enough. More important, I needed his commitment then because my wife was in the midst of her own job negotiations and my decision would greatly affect her options. What the dean suggested, after a few minutes of bantering, was that I agree to come for the $6,000 while he would attempt to get me the extra $500. I told him I couldn't do that and needed a firm commitment from him then for the full $6,500. After a minute or so of silence, he agreed. He then told me, with a smile, that our interchange reminded him of his first job negotiation in 1938.

The situation was somewhat different. He was negotiating for a regular position and it was earlier in the year. The country was also in the grips of a depression. In short, his bargaining position wasn't as strong as mine had been. He had been offered $1,500 by the dean. He was requesting $1,800. Whereas my negotiations had been quite friendly, he told me that during his negotiations the dean became quite vexed despite the fact that she clearly wanted to hire him.[36] When he declined to agree to her offer of $1,500, despite her promise to attempt to get the other $300, she began to lose her temper. Suddenly, however, she caught herself and sat back in her chair. She then leaned across her desk and asked quite calmly, "Mr. Miles, you don't intend to live on what we pay you, do you?"

Her question really summed up quite nicely how many looked upon academic salaries during the prewar years and to some extent the years after the war leading up to Sputnik. Academic salaries, especially for junior faculty members, were seen to be a stipend of sorts rather than a "living." Louis

Mink, one of my undergraduate professors, upon hearing this story told me that at Yale in the mid-1940s it was claimed that assistant professors' salaries were intended to be used to build a personal library and support foreign travel. There was some ambiguity regarding what could and could not be done with an associate professor's salary, but one could not expect to live on one's salary until one was a full professor. I'm not sure how true this was or how widespread the notion, but clearly faculty salaries were comparatively low during this period. Moreover, salaries remained comparatively low until the period of rapid growth beginning in the 1960s.

Unlike the increased costs associated with the funding of physical plants, these increases represented a real increase in cost, not just accounting adjustments. As with some of the increases associated with the physical plant, however, these increases reflected the artificially low costs that prevailed earlier, rather than any sort of illegitimate, nonmarket increase. Nevertheless, as with the increases associated with the physical plant, these salary increases ate into endowment and annual fund resources, leaving less money to underwrite tuition costs.

Unfortunately, from a faculty perspective, whatever real cost increases might have been borne in the late '60s and early '70s , faculty salaries failed to keep pace with inflation during the last twenty years. Whereas the starting salary for a new assistant professor in the mid-'60s at Queens College was nearly $9,000, starting salaries today are around $40,000, which is worth less than $5,000 was worth in the mid-'60s. The 1965 top full-professor salary of approximately $20,000 would convert into a top full-professor salary of over $180,000, which is more than double today's top full-professor salary of approximately $85,000. In fact, my mid-'60s starting salary of $9,000, adjusted for inflation, is worth more than my present top-of-the-scale full-professor salary. In summary, whereas increased salary costs probably contributed to the overall cost pressures experienced by most institutions of higher education during the 1960s and into the early 1970s, they, unlike plant costs, probably make no more demands on resources today than they did forty years ago.

The growth in the number of students attending institutions of higher education has created other types of financial pressures on endowment and annual fund resources, limiting the availability of such funds to subsidize tuition. Perhaps the most significant has been the manner in which increased student numbers have affected scholarships.

On the whole, the "new" students caught up in the pursuit of a college education during the last few decades have been, as a group, financially poorer than the students who had traditionally attended college. This has created a quandary for many institutions, but most notably for the great majority of elite, private schools that have historically prided themselves on their commitment, first and foremost, to academic excellence and to a policy of campus inclusion.

For elite private colleges, selecting the best, forty years ago, meant screening the relatively few students who actually submitted an application to the college. A large percentage of these attended private schools and came from economically secure families. Most of those graduating from public high schools were also relatively well off financially. You had to be relatively well off, or highly motivated, just to be able to finish high school with a college preparatory diploma.[37] Providing scholarship support and campus employment for the relatively few students who could not afford the already subsidized tuition costs did not put an undue strain on most private institutions.

It was not surprising, therefore, that most of these schools adopted what was and is known as an "aid-blind" admission policy in the late '60s and early '70s, when the number of students applying for admissions began to increase. In part, such policies were intended to counteract the charge that only the rich could afford an elite college education, but most institutions were also honestly committed to a policy of inclusion. In effect, what such an aid-blind policy entailed was that anyone who was accepted upon his or her merit would be guaranteed a financial package of a scholarship, loan, and job sufficient to enable him or her to attend the college.

Another major factor leading to increases in enrollments, especially at the more elite colleges, was the trend toward co-education. The pressure to accept women was immense. This meant either reducing dramatically the number of men historically admitted or dramatically increasing overall enrollment. Most institutions elected the second option. While most of the women initially accepted came from the same economically privileged backgrounds as the majority of the men traditionally accepted, their inclusion also created additional financial pressures. The reason for this was that many of these comparatively privileged households had historically sent only their sons to expensive schools. Adding the daughters increased their overall educational financial burden and often entitled them to financial aid.

As the demand for scholarship aid increased, many of these institutions found themselves caught up in a vicious circle. In order to satisfy the growing demand for scholarship aid, a greater proportion of nontuition resources had to be dedicated for scholarships. This left less money available to underwrite tuition costs in general, leading to greater increases in tuition. This, in turn, created yet increased needs for scholarships, not only to cover the increased tuition charges of those already on scholarship but also to provide new scholarships for those no longer able to pay in full the increased tuition charges. This spiral has reached the point where over half the students attending most elite colleges are presently receiving some sort of financial aid. Perhaps more striking is the fact that scholarship aid at most of these elite private institutions is presently equal to a quarter of projected tuition revenue. In many cases it is equal to approximately a third of projected tuition revenue.[38]

The figures for all private colleges as a whole are less dramatic, but even here we find an increase from under 4 percent in 1950 to approximately 20 percent in 1987 in the percentage of scholarship aid compared to tuition income.[39] Today, a modest estimate would place the figure at over 25 percent. The amounts reallocated to financial aid vary from institution to institution, but the drain on annual giving and endowment of such aid has become massive. In many cases financial aid now exceeds total endowment income and eats up practically 75 percent of the combined income from annual giving and endowment income.[40]

Another way of looking at these figures is to note that, based on 1995 data, if scholarship aid was eliminated entirely, tuition costs of many of the presently most expensive and prestigious private schools such as Amherst, Brandeis, California Institute of Technology, Haverford, Smith, Swarthmore, Vassar, and Wellesley, to name a few, could be reduced by over a third.

While public institutions haven't undergone this particular experience, they have been subject to analogous forces that have drawn funds away from general support into more focused scholarship and loan programs. In New York State, for example, where tuition costs have increased dramatically during the last few years, the state has simultaneously been forced to increase funds for financial aid by at least 50 percent. In a number of CUNY colleges, financial aid is equal to over 50 percent of tuition income. And it should be noted that these financial aid figures for both private and public colleges do not include the added institutional expenses associated with administering financial aid offices.

Even admitting the impact of inflation, especially the psychological impact of a thirty-year inflationary shock, and the distortions due to assigning a significant greater proportion of costs to tuition, due to the various reasons described herein, it seems hard to believe that there have not been other substantial changes to cause prices to increase more than might be expected or considered legitimate. The fact is that a number of other things have occurred that have increased costs during the last thirty years. We already referred to one—namely, the increase in faculty salaries during the 1960s. We also noted, however, that from the mid-'70s onward, salaries failed to keep up with inflation, bringing them back to their earlier levels. There are two other developments that seem to have had a real effect: one, an increase in administrative costs, and two, a significant increase in the use of and reliance on technology.

No matter how one tries to juggle the figures, it is pretty clear that both of these factors have generated significant cost increases for higher education. This is somewhat ironic since both the greater use of and reliance on technology and the growth in administrative personnel have been introduced with the promise that they would reduce costs. Moreover, while some commentators within the academy have focused on administrative costs as being the root of the problem, most external critics have failed to accept this view.[41] Similarly, few critics seem eager to attack the increased use of technology. This is true even of those who admit that technology has not reduced costs. The argument seems to be that whatever its cost, technology has brought with it other benefits. The main reason for not wrestling with these factors here, however, is that they are simply not major factors cited by most critics. Put in the context of this book, they are not essential to the "faulty diagnosis." In fact, both of these developments, especially the growth in higher administration, were intended to counteract what were seen to be runaway costs. As such, both of these developments are more appropriately examined in terms of various proposed solutions than in terms of the initial problem. We will later examine each, therefore, in the context of the "false cures."

While technology itself is not normally cited as the villain in increasing the cost of higher education, a number of critics have accused higher educational institutions of tolerating too many unnecessary expensive frills and extras. There is sound evidence, for example, that the increased costs at many of the more elite educational institutions have been due at least in part to a general upgrading of the educational product. Such enrichment initiatives have themselves been motivated by the need of these elite institutions to compete successfully with each other. This argument has been made convincingly by Charles Clotfelter in his book *Buying the Best*, referenced earlier.[42] It should be noted that this is not a case of inefficiency or mismanagement, but rather a case of offering more and charging more. It does raise another issue, however. The apparent economic problems of American higher education may not be due to simple mismanagement of resources but rather to broader mismanagement problems related to the type of product being offered. In short, the problem may not be what we are getting for our money, but what we are being sold.

3

~

Bad Management

Allegations and Reality

Given that charges of fiscal irresponsibility are commonly part of a more encompassing charge of general mismanagement, it is not surprising that American higher education has been subject to such charges.[43] To some extent, this criticism of general mismanagement grows directly out of the criticism of fiscal irresponsibility described in the first chapter. The argument, basically, is that the excessive cost of American higher education is due to a large degree to a failure to impose the market management principles used in the corporate sector. In this context, a number of specific educational management practices and principles are commonly criticized. As a consequence, simply refuting the charge of fiscal mismanagement, as was done in the previous chapter, doesn't in and of itself relieve higher education from these additional accusations.

Since principles generally guide practices, we will begin with several presumed management principles of higher education that historically have been most commonly criticized. We will then move on to examine certain practices that have been attacked as products of these principles. As might be expected, there is a good deal of overlap among the various principles, as well as some blurring of the principle/practice distinction. It is also necessary, in the case of both principles and practices, to determine not only whether these principles and practices have the negative consequences that are assumed, but also whether they, in fact, prevail. As we shall see, while most of the principles and the practices criticized do flourish within academia, they are seldom as significant as commonly assumed. More important is the fact that they tend not to have the negative consequences that they are alleged to produce.

So what are these iniquitous management principles of American higher education? Nine are commonly offered:

1. Academic institutions have relied too heavily on leadership selected from within the institution.

This criticism is most commonly directed at the manner in which lower and intermediate management are selected, because for decades college presidents have usually been externally selected. In contrast, departmental chairs have nearly always and academic deans have historically been selected from within the institution. The assumed implication of this criticism is that internally selected chairs and deans can't lead because, having come from the ranks, they lack the appropriate vision and perspective required to transcend the present situation. In addition, it is similarly assumed that they are normally too beholden to their old colleagues to exert any real authority over them and, moreover, are unwilling to force them to change in any way.

2. Academic institutions have failed to ensure sufficient turnover of senior management.

This criticism is closely linked to the previous one and similarly assumes that good management requires a continual influx of new blood and new ideas. The thrust of this criticism, however, is not that leadership is drawn from within so much as that, once selected, chairs and deans, and even presidents, stay too long. The two criticisms, while analytically distinct, are closely related.

Finding suitable leaders within an organization is not easy. As a consequence, there is a tendency to hold on to someone once selected, even if only because most people are more comfortable with a "devil they know rather than a devil they don't know." In addition, if a chair or dean was initially selected from within, that person is likely to return to the faculty if he or she is replaced. If a chair or a dean elects to step down voluntarily, this normally causes no problem, but if that person is forced to do so, negative repercussions will likely follow.

To complicate matters more, an internal chair or dean normally was selected, often even pressured to accept the position, by the very same people who will now have to replace him or her. There is a tendency, consequently, to leave leadership selected from the ranks in place longer than leaders selected externally. Whatever the reason, the complaint is that the policy of keeping administrators on for long periods of time results in a lackluster administration.

3. Academic institutions excessively limit the power and control granted to management. *In academic parlance this principle often reads:* **Academic institutions are overly committed to the principle of shared governance.**

This criticism is closely connected to the first two. Here, however, the focus is not on the methods by which leaders are selected and maintained, but rather on the powers formally granted them. The charge is that in institutions of higher education, the rank and file, that is, the faculty, is empowered with too much authority. In some cases this charge is intended to cover everything from curriculum matters to hiring and promotion. In other cases, the charge deals more specifically with traditional management issues such as hiring, promotion, allocation of funds, and organizational goals, while ceding to faculty curriculum and more limited academic issues. The thrust of this criticism isn't that administrators are unwilling to lead (the essence of the first two criticisms), but rather that they don't have the power to do so.

4. Academic institutions are too wedded to traditional ways of doing things.

This charge follows from the first three and is intended to cover a wide range of more specific criticisms. By and large, the thrust of this accusation is that too much reliance is placed on doing things the way they have always been done. It is claimed that this is due not only to the presence of an inbred administration, but also to a pervasive tendency to look for potential drawbacks to any innovation. There is a fear of change. Coupled with the principle of shared governance noted earlier, this means that whenever a new procedure or process is suggested, someone, somewhere will raise some objection related to some problem that occurred sometime in the past when someone else had attempted to do something similar, and it didn't work.

5. Academic institutions lack sufficient accountability.

This criticism, like the previous one, is related to the charge of too much shared governance. Here the issue is final responsibility. Since nearly everyone has a say in what is and what is not to be done, it is difficult if not impossible to assign proper responsibility for failures or, for that matter, proper credit for successes. This structural problem is further compounded by a tendency to avoid closure through continual analysis and discussion. Because it is difficult to get the collective to decide whether a particular scheme has or has not worked, it is nearly impossible to establish accountability. You can't hold anyone accountable for something until there is minimally some agreement on what, in fact, occurred.

6. Academics, in principle, are negatively disposed to establishing a meaningful reward and punishment system.

This charge is closely tied to the last two criticisms but focuses on another tenet as well. Whether because of a general ambivalence toward materialistic goods or due to some other reason, academics tend to avoid using the pressures of rewards and punishments commonly used in other organizations. Many institutions of higher education have no system of merit pay whatsoever. Those that do, tend to have, at most, highly anemic systems as compared to those used in the corporate world. Where bonuses and pay raises for exceptional work can equal a quarter to a half of one's annual salary in the corporate world, merit raises in academia seldom amount to more than a few extra percents of salary. There is admittedly a highly developed system governing promotions, but this system is related almost exclusively to the academic activities of the faculty. Their institutional loyalties and contributions play, at most, a small part in this promotional system.

7. Academic institutions privilege individual interests over collective interest to a degree that harms the institution.

This charge is clearly foreshadowed by a number of criticisms already made. Here, however, the failure of the institution to establish firmer principles of accountability, utilize a more robust system of rewards and punishments, and limit shared governance is tied directly to the preference given the interests and needs of the individual members of the institution over the interests of the institution per se. This principle is often seen as hindering the institution's ability to properly control the behavior of its members, especially when it comes to issues such as academic freedom and academic free speech.

8. Academic institutions are committed to principles and practices that deliberately maintain an inherently weak administrative structure.

9. Academic institutions refuse to implement market principles that have been proven successful in the corporate world.

Charges 8 and 9, in effect, sum up the first seven charges made.

While it would be possible to expand this list, these nine charges adequately cover the substance of what I have labeled the attack on principles. While these charges have been used to decry the general condition of institutions of higher education, they have also been used to attack a wide range of specific institutional practices. A number of these practices deserve special attention since they have not only come under repeated attack, but have also been used to document and justify the more general criticism lodged against academic management principles. At minimum, five practices need to be noted.[44]

ACADEMIC TENURE

Few academic practices have been more fiercely and universally attacked as academic tenure.[45] The most commonly voiced characterization of academic tenure, especially from those who are most critical of it, is that it forces academic institutions to keep faculty members who are no longer doing their job. Others complain that even in those situations where a faculty member may not be a complete loss, tenure prohibits the institution from replacing a mediocre faculty member with a more promising younger faculty person, who can be hired for less money. This type of job security, it is argued, has the added negative effect of enabling tenured faculty members to perform below their full capabilities.

While there are times when these complaints have some merit—sometimes it would be possible, for example, to hire a younger, more energetic person for less money—the criticism tends to ignore the many offsetting advantages to tenure. The simple fact is that most critics who recommend elimination of tenure do not understand what tenure really is or how it works.

Academic tenure is a formal commitment by the granting institution to the faculty member receiving tenure to guarantee the holder of tenure his or her position under most circumstances. There are cases, however, when this guarantee does not hold. Financial exigencies, that is, the lack of funds to cover salaries, generally release institutions from such commitments. Admittedly complex procedural rules normally govern this process to ensure that such claimed fiscal exigencies are real. Procedures also exist to ensure that such things as seniority are respected. Tenure obligations, however, cannot force institutions of higher learning to go into bankruptcy, as some critics would have us believe.

Various behaviors on the part of the faculty member may also be used to divest that person of his or her position. Most people have heard of the concept *moral turpitude* that is built into most tenure agreements, whereby a faculty member can be dismissed for such things as sexual misconduct with students, fraud, drunkenness in class, and so on. Certain less egregious job performance–related transgressions are also grounds for termination. A faculty member who fails to attend class, who treats students inappropriately, or who acts and speaks nonprofessionally in class can be brought up for dismissal. Again, removing a faculty member for such reasons is never easy, but it can be and has been done.

While critics of tenure are prone to note that academic tenure may force institutions to retain the services of a faculty member whom they would prefer to remove, these critics generally ignore the very strict standards and requirements necessary to obtain tenure in the first place. Basically, in all institutions, tenure is not granted until after a trial period that can only be called a period of servitude and that normally lasts seven years—the same period of time that Jacob had to labor for Rachel's hand. Yet whereas Jacob agreed to work for Lot seven years as part of a contractual agreement guaranteeing that Rachel would be his afterward, nontenured faculty members are forced to labor with no such guarantee. In fact, in many cases they do so knowing that the probabilities are greater that they will not get tenure than that they will.

What makes this situation even more perilous is that in nearly all cases if they do not receive tenure, they lose their jobs completely. Moreover, if after being turned down for tenure at one institution, they are fortunate enough to get a new job, the whole process starts over again—although the second job's apprenticeship period may be reduced by a year or two. Many academics have to go through this process three or more times before they receive tenure. Others keep moving from institution to institution without ever receiving tenure during their entire professional career. In summary, while tenure might offer an added degree of job security, the system that provides it does no such thing. If anything, overall job security in institutions of higher education is more fragile than in most other institutions.

There is another immense institutional advantage to tenure that critics of tenure nearly always fail to mention. Tenure is an amazingly cheap fringe benefit. The critics of tenure often complain of tenure's cost by pointing out that many institutions are stuck with paying more to nonproductive, or less productive, tenured faculty members than they would have to pay for younger, more promising, nontenured faculty members. What they fail to acknowledge is that the system allows educational institutions to maintain the services of more highly productive faculty members for much less money than they would have to pay if there were no tenure.

How is it that educational institutions can hire highly trained experts with more academic training than lawyers, accountants, and even physicians for less than half and often for less than a third of what these other experts are paid? How do they get these young scholars to work the many hours necessary not only to prepare and teach their classes, but to pursue their own research agendas for less than most first-year medical interns receive and only a fraction of the salaries that starting lawyers receive? How do they get them to do this for seven or more years while maintaining them on such comparatively low salaries? The answer, in most cases, is by the hope for tenure.

The pressure to continue to work long and hard hours for little remuneration, moreover, is not over even if tenure is obtained. Tenure brings with it a degree of job security, but it seldom brings much in the form of financial reward. To obtain more money, a junior faculty person needs to be promoted. In many institutions, tenure and initial promotion are linked. This is reflected in the familiar expression *up or out,* which means either you receive tenure and are promoted or you are dismissed. Promotion to associate professor, which often accompanies tenure, however, is only one step in the process. One must still be promoted to full professor to reach one's full earning power as an academic.

The situation has actually become even more difficult in recent years, with more institutions separating promotion to associate professor from tenure decisions. Rather than be promoted with tenure, junior faculty are expected to put in a few more years of servitude before being promoted to associate professor or, in other cases, accept promotion without tenure. In either situation, there are still the years of "servitude" necessary for promotion to full professor. And as if this were not enough, a growing number of institutions have recently instituted subsequent reviews and a promotion process for full professor before such professors can reach the top of the pay scale.

Taken together, these various post-tenure review procedures can amount to fifteen to twenty years of service at below market rates before a faculty member has achieved what might be called his or her economic emancipation. Even then, the salary is likely to be only a fraction of what professionals in other fields with similar credentials are paid. As my wife has often remarked, "They think it's a part-time job, so they pay you a part-time salary."

What this means is that although a senior full professor who elects to work less later in life may be shortchanging his or her institution, this professor has already worked for twenty or more years at significantly less salary than he or she would have earned elsewhere. When this fact and the others noted previously are coupled with the statistic that the great majority of senior faculty members continue to earn their salaries, it becomes clear that the economic gains associated with tenure clearly outweigh the occasional costs. It is a classic example of an unfunded fringe benefit. Admittedly, tenure is not based on the same market principles that govern most employment contracts in the private sector. On the other hand, I would argue that most for-profit organizations would be thrilled if their employment system were as economically efficient as is the tenure system of American higher education.

SABBATICAL LEAVES

After tenure, sabbatical leaves probably receive the most criticism as an inefficient, wasteful academic practice. Again, as with tenure, there appears to be a good deal of misinformation regarding what the practice actually entails. First, as the name indicates, a faculty member must normally first work for that particular institution for seven years. Second, sabbaticals are generally restricted to tenured faculty. I have known many academics who have taught for close to twenty years at various institutions before finally becoming eligible for their first sabbatical. Moreover, while some institutions allow tenured faculty to take sabbatical leaves as a right, this is presently the exception rather than the rule. In a growing number of institutions, sabbatical leaves must be applied for and justified. That is, the faculty member is required to present a detailed proposal indicating how he or she will spend his or her sabbatical leave and how it will benefit the institution.

This is usually interpreted to mean that the faculty member not only must present a fairly explicit research agenda but must relate this agenda to his or her teaching objectives. Often, faculty members have to provide outside evaluations of the sabbatical plan and apply for external funding. Even when there is no formal requirement to seek external funding, such funding has become necessary because many if not most institutions now do not fully fund sabbatical leaves. Rather than enabling faculty members to take time off at full pay, more institutions now put faculty members on sabbatical leave at half pay, expecting them to obtain additional funds externally.

Even with these limitations, it must be admitted that few nonacademic institutions regularly allow a substantial number of their employees to take a year off every seven years, even at half pay. Moreover, any sabbatical, even one at half pay, would appear to constitute a fairly expensive faculty benefit. In fact, this is not the case. The reason for this is that in most cases little, if any, additional cost is incurred to replace the faculty members who go on sabbatical leave. In the great majority of these cases, the half salary saved is generally more than sufficient to hire part-time substitute faculty. Many institutions actually save money when a senior faculty member goes on sabbatical since they are able to hire part-time adjunct replacements for significantly less than the half salary saved. Even when faculty members receive full pay on sabbatical, the cost for their replacements tends to be quite minimal. In addition, the faculty members on sabbatical often do have external grants, which not only further lessen the salary costs to the institution, but may even provide overhead funds from the grant to the institution.[46]

Whereas initially sabbatical leaves were intended to provide faculty members with time to lie fallow and rejuvenate themselves, few faculty members are allowed this respite today. As indicated previously, the pressures on faculty members to pursue their own research and to publish are very heavy. For the faculty of today, sabbatical leaves are seldom times for relaxation. Rather, sabbaticals are times when faculty members are expected to get on with their own work. It is permissible and expected that a faculty member on sabbatical leave may take some personal time off, but most of the time he or she is expected to be working. Moreover, when this work results in publishable material, which is the general expectation, the institution benefits as well as the faculty member. In short, a sabbatical leave may entail a break from teaching, but it seldom converts into a break from work. Similarly, although a sabbatical leave is granted to a given individual, the fact that the institution expects to benefit from the leave and others are expected to pick up any slack created, reveals that such leaves serve institutional interests as much as individual interests. Here again, the costs and benefits are not governed by familiar market principles, but there is no evidence that anything is being given away.

RELEASED TIME FOR FACULTY
FROM TEACHING TO ENGAGE IN RESEARCH

A third academic practice that has lately come under regular attack relates to the way faculty time and energy are allocated. As noted in the first chapter, faculty members seldom teach as many courses per semester as the number of courses that students are expected to take. In some institutions, faculty members may average no more than six hours a week in the classroom. Even adding preparation time, advisement, committee work, and so on, they are left with a significant amount of time to pursue their individual research. This is also true, if more modestly, for faculty members who teach nine, twelve, or even fifteen hours a week. (Heavy class loads normally entail teaching multiple sections of the same course, which cuts down on preparation time.) It is this research time that is often criticized as wasteful. The complaint is not only that the time could be better spent in the classroom, but also that most of the research produced tends be of little value. Here again, we have an example of criticism based on a mistaken view of what a particular academic practice is meant to accomplish, as well as an oversimplified notion of how different types of work efforts are to be accounted.

During the last ten to twenty years, there has been increased concern over the conflict between teaching and research in higher education, with most critics lamenting the attention given to research at the apparent cost to teaching. In fact, a movement in education directed at correcting this situation has arisen in the last few years.[4/] As important as teaching clearly is, I would suggest that insofar as there is a teaching problem in higher education, it has little to do with the traditional role of research in higher education. (That a problem might exist due to the way research has lately been refined is another matter to which we will return.)[48]

Nearly all of this concern and criticism, however, fails to take into account why higher education faculty members have traditionally been expected to engage in individual research and scholarship. Such research and scholarship were never intended as ends in themselves. Moreover, they were never intended to be alternatives to teaching. Rather, they were seen as an absolute prerequisite for adequate college and university teaching.

College and university education was not intended merely to be a continuation of high school education, in which students acquired specific information and learned specific intellectual skills. The purpose of higher education was to prepare students to accept more important leadership and managerial positions. Essential to nearly all of these positions, whether in business, the professions, or education itself, was the need for critical and creative thinking. While it was hoped that college and university education might impart some useful knowledge and skills, the key to a good liberal arts and sciences education was the ability to problem-solve and frame questions.

It was particularly this type of creative thinking that the faculty was expected to impart to students. It was understood that in order for faculty members to be able to do this, they had to be engaged in ongoing original research and scholarship. In short, faculty members were expected to *keep up* with what was happening in their fields, not in order to publish new research but to ensure that they could honestly convey what original thinking entailed.

Admittedly, the emphasis was and remains somewhat different in major research institutions. These institutions, however, make up a small minority of higher education institutions in the United States. Moreover, even in these research institutions, one of the major goals is to train new researchers by exposing them to the practices of senior researchers. This learning is of central importance, if for no other reason than because it is understood that very little research will likely be beneficial in any significant way. If a baseball batter who gets a hit in one out of three times at bat is an all-star, a medical research team that produces something of significance in one out of a thousand attempts will probably be awarded a Nobel prize. In the other physical sciences, the social sciences, and the humanities, the probability of research generating publicly recognized useful results is, if anything, less. To condemn most academic research and scholarship because it normally fails to generate useful results is simply to misunderstand what the objectives of such research and scholarship were and are.[49]

ACADEMIC FREEDOM AND FREE SPEECH

If the critics of American higher education find tenure, sabbatical leaves, and released time for research and scholarship wasteful, they often find the tolerance of different and deviant academic opinions and speech abhorrent. In fact, more often than not, such differing and deviant opinions and speech provoke the attacks on tenure and research in the first place. The critics can't understand why or how a faculty member who expresses such opinions can be allowed to stay on the faculty, or how the institution can in any way lend its support to *research and scholarship* that is associated with such opinions and/or views.

Here again, the problem seems to be one of failing to understand the function that such opinions play or, more correctly, that the *right to express* such opinions plays in higher education. American higher education was never intended to merely convey accepted wisdom and truths to the next generation. Students are expected to be able to think critically and to reach thoughtful conclusions on their own. This requires that they not be coddled when they confront and evaluate different ideas. Higher education needs faculty members who can formulate and articulate new and often unattractive ideas.

Faculty members who are allowed to express these ideas do so under already existing strict rules. While they can argue for their positions publicly, they are not allowed to proselytize in the classroom. Moreover, their opinions are subject to the same criteria and evidence that apply in general. Some students may be *misled* for a while by extreme and perhaps even faulty views, but most of them learn through exposure how better to evaluate and judge such views. Institutions of higher learning, by ensuring that this process can occur within a highly controlled context, fulfill an extremely valuable social service. They should not be condemned, but instead thanked, for defending what has come to be known as academic freedom. Few, if any, other social institutions are capable of fulfilling this important social and civic mission.

SHARED FACULTY GOVERNANCE

While shared governance—a governance structure that gives faculty a major voice in governance issues—is seldom explicitly and publicly targeted by critics of higher education, it is perhaps the single most criticized aspect of higher education by nonacademic institutional insiders. Such insiders include members of boards of trustees and overseers, senior administrators, and a host of ex-academic consultants. When one gets through reviewing their various criticisms, which generally cover everything from weak academic leadership, indulged faculty, and tenure to sabbaticals and excessive academic free speech, one finds generally a deep resentment against the power that the faculty maintains over everything from curriculum and accreditation criteria and promotion and tenure procedures the selection of departmental chairs and deans and long-range institutional goals. As a trustee of one college once said to me, "The damn faculty are everywhere. You can't do anything around here without them putting their nose into it."

Here we are perhaps getting to the root of what many perceive to be the problem of higher education. Faculties have historically had considerably more power within their institutions than do personnel in analogous positions in other institutions. What nearly all critics of this situation fail to recognize is that empowering faculty has produced a remarkably efficient system of governance, given the issues and tasks that confront higher education. A good case can be made, in fact, that the practice has much to recommend it to other institutions. Even a fairly cursory comparison of the strengths and weaknesses of what might be called traditional academic governance systems support this position.[50]

The first thing that needs to be appreciated when examining the traditional organizational structure of most institutions of higher education is how simple and nonhierarchical it is. Most American colleges and universities have historically had few administrators. A typical college of 1,000 to 2,000 students in the 1960s might had have a faculty of 80 to 200 members, with a support staff of another 100 to 200 people. This workforce was officially supervised by a senior management group that normally included little more than a president, a dean of faculty, a dean of students, perhaps a dean of freshman, one or two senior financial personnel, and perhaps three or four other senior management people in charge of such things as admissions, buildings and grounds, athletics, and so on.

If one broke out the nonacademic staff and perused only the academic staff, one was likely to be left with little more than the president and a dean of faculty in official supervisory roles. Augmenting these two, of course, one would also find ten to twenty departmental chairs, but these chairs were nearly always members of the faculty and supported, if not actually selected, by their academic colleagues. In turn, these departmental chairs normally saw it as their role to champion their departments and colleagues as much as to advocate senior-management policy.

It doesn't take much figuring to realize that such a system invested relatively little into supervisory personnel. If this type of system is to work, however, it is essential that the faculty as a whole be willing to take on what is normally considered supervisory responsibility. Given the issues that such responsibility covers within higher education institutions, such shared responsibility proves to be not only economically and administratively efficient but required by the nature of these issues. More specifically, academic decisions tend to focus on issues of curriculum, pedagogy, and evaluation. Such decisions not only require a high degree of expertise, but this expertise varies from one academic department to the next.

Expertise is required not only to resolve curriculum issues—which subjects and texts are most appropriate for which courses, what is the best sequencing of courses, what requirements should be established as prerequisites for different courses, what the requirements should be for certification as a major in a given field, and so on—but also to determine the type of staff required to teach these courses. The same high level of expertise is required to evaluate the efforts and work of this staff. No academic dean, let alone president, can be expected to have the expertise to be able to function in such a supervisory role for twenty or more departments.

The practice of empowering the faculty is not only necessary, it is economically highly efficient. While from one perspective, empowering faculty members may appear to give them an advantage, from another perspective the empowerment represents a heavy burden. In most other institutions supervisory personnel are given high salaries and significant authority to do these things. Here, faculty members are expected to do them as part of their regular jobs of teaching and carrying on their scholarship and research. In order to ensure the commitment and time required by such self-management, the institution needs to grant the faculty commensurate rights. If faculty members are to monitor and enforce institutional expectations, then they need to participate in the process whereby these expectations are determined. This is what shared academic governance is all about.

It is somewhat ironic to note that while academic institutions have come under increased attack for what is often criticized as unmanageable shared governance systems, there is a growing interest in the private economic sector to modify organizational structures in a way that will give those lower in the hierarchy greater power and influence. This is all part of a general move to decentralize institutional authority. While the need to tap into the expertise of those further down the line is noted in these nonacademic situations, the main reasons given for pursuing such a course are to maximize flexibility and to increase workers' institutional commitment and loyalties. It is also recognized that workers further down the line are often in a better position than higher management to see emerging problems as well as possible solutions. In short, while faculties are being criticized for hindering upper management initiatives and plans, many in the private economic sector are realizing that increased input from below will not only produce better solutions to many problems but can also protect an institution from making grave errors.

It is important to acknowledge that shared governance has not only been inexpensive and functionally efficient but has also served to enhance what sociologists call social solidarity. By this, I mean that it has served to enhance institutional morale and loyalty, which is not a trivial accomplishment. Academics tend to be highly egocentric. This is neither surprising nor necessarily inappropriate, given that in order to successfully meet their academic responsibilities, they must be engaged with and pursue their individual muse. Academics are not hired to get along with their colleagues or to grapple with institutional problems. They are hired to undertake individual research and to share their insights and knowledge with their students. The only way it is possible to seduce most faculty members into becoming interested in the well-being of the institution as a whole is through a sense of shared ownership of the institution.

The fact that most, if not all, faculty members tend to take a proprietary interest in their institutions is not the problem that some critics would lead us to believe. It is true that such proprietary interests make faculty members loath to change traditional practices. It similarly makes them resistant to external suggestions, no matter how commendable these may appear. And God protect those who attempt to infringe on faculty members' historical prerogatives, be they in curricular, pedagogical, or personnel matters. The positive side of this *ownership,* however, is not only institutional loyalty but also a keen understanding of a wide range of hidden pitfalls and unrecognized interconnections that can, if ignored, undermine even the noblest initiative. In short, faculty resistance to change is not usually counterproductive. Faculty skepticism, more often than not, turns out to be a healthy reality check.

As someone who has spent most of the last decade in various administrative roles, I clearly do not believe that all faculty resistance and skepticism is constructive or useful. On the other hand, it clearly isn't always destructive. Whether faculty skepticism does more good or more harm when it comes to evaluating and implementing innovations is really beside the point. The fact is, in academia periods of significant change are the exception, not the rule. And during the normal day-to-day activities that constitute the life history of most academic institutions, it is certain that the loyalty and commitment of faculty, the sense of ownership, plays a highly constructive role. Without this sense of ownership, most academic institutions would rapidly disintegrate.

It is equally true that when change is needed, faculty members must be willing to move forward on their own. Quite simply, no existent supervisory structure can force them to move. Here again, without a sense of owner-ship—no matter how arduous it may be to generate—nothing will change.

Some people might claim that this is an exaggeration. It could be argued that most faculty members go about their daily activities quite oblivious to their peers and even their students. Such a view would appear to be consis-tent with the previous comments that most faculty members tend, of neces-sity, to be egocentric. Even egocentric types of work, however, do not occur in a vacuum. The most singleminded faculty members need to believe that their efforts will be and can be appreciated by others, even if these others number only a few. The peer review aspect of shared faculty governance plays a central role in maintaining faculty confidence in how work is evalu-ated. Here again, the system does not always work. Few academic institu-tions have not experienced faculty members' complaints that they have been mistreated by colleagues who do not properly appreciate or understand their work. Without the peer-based system that has historically been employed, however, such complaints would multiply geometrically.

While other positive aspects of shared faculty governance could be noted, enough have been presented, I believe, to justify the conclusion that while the traditional management principles and practices of higher education have their shortcomings, they clearly don't merit the scorn that critics have showered upon them. Moreover, as noted, these principles and practices are often quite sensitive to what could be called market factors. This raises the same question noted earlier when we discovered a similar unjustified attack on the financial status of higher education, namely, why such an accusation should not only be so common but so generally accepted. It is to this issue that we now turn.

4

~

So Why the Bad Rap?

Multiple Products and Multiple Markets

If the management principles and practices of American higher education are as sound and sensible as the previous chapter would suggest, why are so many people critical of them? If tenure, sabbatical leaves, the emphasis on research, faculty governance, and the like aren't inherently inefficient, why do so many people feel that something is fundamentally wrong with higher education?

Obviously, one answer cannot cover all situations. I would suggest, however, that most hostile attitudes are grounded in one overriding judgment, though this judgment takes a variety of specific forms. The judgment is that American higher education is providing the wrong product to the wrong audience. This belief, in turn, is based upon assumptions regarding who should be served by higher education and what they should receive. When it comes to specifics, the whole subject gets quite complex since even the most ardent critics normally believe that there are different legitimate clientele. Different clientele, however, should receive different types of education. Given that all of these judgments and assumptions are politically and ideologically charged and hence highly controversial, it is perhaps not surprising that most critics prefer to focus on fiscal and organizational mismanagement.

To get a sense of just how intense the debate over the proper role of higher education has become, one need only glance at such books as William Bennett's *The De-Valuing of America,* Bill Readings's *The University in Ruins,* Gary Nelson's *Manifesto of a Tenured Radical,* or George Dennis O'Brien's *All the Half-Truths about American Higher Education.* For a less polemical review of this debate, which is commonly called the *culture war,* I would recommend Donald Kennedy's *Academic Duty.*

That American higher education should have become the political battle-ground it has, is in and of itself an interesting historical twist. American education, especially American higher education, was the darling of both the political right and the political left for most of the country's history. If America was proclaimed the land of opportunity, the great melting pot, it was American education that was championed as the means for achieving this goal. Education was perceived as providing otherwise deprived individuals with the knowledge and skills that were necessary to achieve success. It was also seen as fostering the values and ideals needed to form a healthy democratic nation. As Theodore White reveals in his book *In Search of History*,[51] from the Civil War through World War II, education was America's welfare system. And the grand mix of American higher education, which included everything from the Ivy League schools to various night colleges, including night law schools and other graduate programs, was perhaps the acme of this system.[52]

So what happened to turn so many political activists, especially those with more conservative views, against American higher education? A number of things. I would emphasize five: (1) a significant increase, both in numbers and percentages, in people attending institutions of higher education, which in and of itself undermined the historic *gatekeeper* role of higher education;[53] (2) a significant shift in the ethnic, racial, gender, and class characteristics of those attending institutions of higher education, which threatened the *identity* of higher education;[54] (3) a reordering of academic skills required of those attending college, which questioned the value of previously acquired skills;[55] (4) an exponential growth in the accepted academic canon of books, art forms, ideas, data, information, and theoretical orientations in nearly every academic field, which questioned what counts as knowledge and education;[56] and (5) an ideological shift that privileged students' educational interests and demands over those of the faculty and the larger society, which challenged traditional hierarchies.[57]

Though these issues are interrelated, for clarity's sake it makes sense to attempt, at least initially, to deal with them individually. The focus will be on the major questions, noted earlier, of who should attend institutions of higher learning and what should they learn once they are there.

Fifty years ago only a small proportion of what might be considered the college-age (eighteen to twenty-two years old) population attended liberal arts and sciences colleges. These people tended to be male and primarily from the upper middle and upper classes. Their education was seen as a rite de passage preparing them for their adult role as corporate, professional, and civic leaders. In the case of women, who constituted a distinct minority, motherhood coupled with civic service was also acceptable. The education students received was highly structured, with much similarity from institution to institution. The curriculum stressed accepted *classics* of Western civilization. The less privileged were welcome, though their numbers were limited, but the overriding objective was to produce *gentlemen* and *gentlewomen,* regardless of their origin.

With the end of World War II, the demographics of higher education began to change as thousands of veterans entered colleges and universities on the GI Bill. The curriculum, however, remained very much the same as did the basic objective, namely, to produce future leaders.

In the '60s, the numbers and demographic mix of students attending institutions of higher learning went through yet another change. Whereas prewar attendance percentages for college-age cohorts tended to remain under 10 percent and postwar percentages grew to over 20 percent, the late '60s and the 1970s found over 40 percent of these age cohorts attending some form of higher education institution. Whereas these students were once almost always white and predominantly male, the college population of the '60s and '70s was increasingly diverse ethnically and racially, as well as increasingly female. In terms of who was attending, higher education had clearly changed. How people responded to this change differed.

Some critics, predominantly from the political right, argued, and continue to argue, that American higher education was becoming debased. These critics claimed that too many students without the proper skills and credentials were being accepted. The tone of these criticisms, however, often indicated concern for more than credentials and skills. The increased numbers, in and of themselves, seemed to bother many people insofar as they threatened higher education's historic gatekeeping role in selecting those destined to assume future leadership positions in society. Publicly expressing such elitist views, no matter how strongly held, however, is apt to be seen as politically incorrect, insofar as it goes counter to the American ideals of inclusion and equality. It is easier to attack those fostering such inclusive practices by charging general mismanagement. Charges that characterize management as generally inept, prone to fuzzy thinking, and lacking rigorous standards have the added advantage of implicitly attacking inclusiveness by first associating standards and rigor with intellectual excellence, then selectivity, and only then, out of necessity, elitism.

Critics on the political left, in contrast, tended to argue that institutions of higher education, even with growth in numbers, were and are still wedded to the past and an outdated elitist philosophy.[58] Rather than arguing that too many people are now allowed to attend institutions of higher education, they believe that too many people are still being kept out. The problem isn't that the demographics of the student body are changing but that they aren't changing quickly enough. Leftist critics further argue that the issue isn't a lack of academic skills on the part of these new students, but academia's irrational adherence to outmoded criteria and a failure to adjust and revise curricula to keep pace with the changing world. Here again, however, it is often easier to formulate criticisms attacking antiquated management principles rather than articulate a more explicit political agenda.

As indicated earlier, these critics—both from the left and the right—are normally as concerned with what is taught as with those who are taught. One only has to think of Allan Bloom's book *The Closing of the American Mind*[59] and the many responses, both pro and con, that it has generated to grasp how extensive and intense this *culture war* has become. Should Western civilization be privileged in American colleges? In literature courses should Third World, racially diverse, gay, and other "nontraditional" authors be given equal representation to more traditionally taught authors such as Shakespeare, Milton, Goethe, and so forth?

The controversy over what institutions of higher learning should be teaching, however, goes far beyond what should or should not be accepted as the liberal education canon. Decisions regarding what students should read and learn are directly related to the assumed purpose of their education. Is the purpose of higher education to select leaders? Is it to prepare students for employment? It is to produce better-informed citizens? Clearly, how one answers these questions will influence how one decides questions bearing on curricula issues.

While all of these questions, as well as questions regarding who should attend college and what they should study, are deserving of attention, it is important to realize that there are no fiscally or administratively correct answers. All sorts of people for all sorts of reasons may not like the way our institutions of higher learning are being managed, but this does not prove mismanagement. Given the political sensitivity of these issues, however, it does explain why some people might be more comfortable framing their attacks in fiscal and management terms.

The situation, and consequently the task of distinguishing the various criticisms made, is further complicated by the fact that in these debates and discussions political lines often become crossed. In the debates emphasizing that higher education should consider the future employment needs of students, for example, we often find splits among the various camps in the curricula debate. Some—generally white male business leaders educated prior to the 1970s, with both fiscal and social conservative leanings—argue vehemently for both greater employment relevancy and a traditional curricula. Others, generally younger, more demographically diverse, and "market oriented," are equally, if not more, committed to a policy that prepares students for future employment, but they want to do so through a radically transformed curriculum that is less theoretical, more inclusive, and more practical.

On the other hand, proponents on both sides of the curricula/cultural debate argue strongly against a greater emphasis on employment implications. Some people who defend a more traditional education argue that it is not the job of higher education to prepare students for the workplace. That is the job of trade school or graduate school. The job of higher education is to produce critical and informed thinkers. The best—in fact, the only—way to do this is to require that students be exposed to a traditional liberal education that emphasizes the literary, historical, and political classics of Western civilization.

Others, who likewise reject transforming higher education into employment training, argue quite differently. They argue that the purpose of higher education is to radicalize students and enable them to transform society when they graduate, not merely to give them skills that will allow them to find a job. This requires, however, that they be exposed to a significantly different curriculum than the curriculum of the 1940s and 1950s. Today's students, these critics argue, require familiarity with non-Western ideas and need to be trained in critical thinking.[60]

Again, as with the earlier proponents, these critics often hesitate to articulate their views explicitly, which generally serves to provoke conflict. It is easier simply to criticize the way things are presently done and those in charge; fiscal and management issues often provide an easy vehicle for doing this.

For many people there are other advantages to attacking those in charge. Simply put, for a variety of different reasons, a number of people believe that those in charge, whoever they may be, shouldn't be in charge. This situation often takes the form of an alumnus or alumna criticizing the present leadership of his or her own school. As an active class representative for my own alma mater, I can attest to the fact that a year doesn't pass without a classmate or other alumnus expressing such criticism to me. While the school, as in my case, is more likely to be a private institution, public institutions are subject to the same assault. In the case of public institutions, however, such alumni assaults are often augmented by similar assaults from taxpayers who take a proprietary interest in "their" school. In all of these situations, the frustration that critics experience regarding campus policies is exacerbated by their sense of ownership and entitlement when it comes to deciding what should be done. This often serves to redirect their criticism toward those in charge rather than at specific educational policies and practices.

Frustration at being ignored can and often does supplant criticism of policy and practices. In my various academic roles—class agent, fundraiser, faculty member, chair, and dean—associated with a number of different institutions, I have personally experienced such situations on numerous occasions. Criticism of a particular policy or practice is made. The response, whatever it might be, is seen as insufficient. This lack of response then becomes the issue. Rather than dealing directly with this experienced slight, however (I have concluded that most people are uncomfortable in responding to what they experience as a slight), it is common for critics to redirect their anger back into their original complaint, but with more animus against the institutional leadership. Put slightly differently, the problem becomes one of leadership rather than of particular policies and practices.

One concrete personal experience might help to illustrate this general pattern. Some years ago, a successful classmate who had been a generous supporter of our alma mater called me to vent his concern over aspects of the current curriculum. In the course of our conversation, he indicated that he intended to raise the issue with the college president, members of the board of trustees, and some faculty members. He was a successful graduate and known by pretty much everyone on campus. To make a long story short, and it was quite a long story, after venting his feelings with a number of different people on campus over a period of approximately three months, my classmate was, in effect, told that curriculum wasn't his business.

Not surprisingly, he wasn't pleased. Somewhat more surprising, at least initially to me, he refused to participate in the next fundraising campaign. In discussing this with him, I took great pains to review his initial complaint and the various reasons given him by various people for not only supporting the particular curriculum items to which he objected, but also the particular process whereby these curriculum decisions were made. His response took me aback. He acknowledged that he was still upset by the present curriculum, but this was not why he had decided not to contribute. He was not going to contribute because, ignoring the curriculum issue, he had concluded that he no longer had any confidence in the present leadership. With that, he proceeded to criticize a number of fiscal and administrative decisions taken during the last few years. What was noteworthy about his list was that he had never mentioned one of the items previously. In fact, when *I* had complained about some of these items, he had previously told me that the board and the president probably had their reasons for doing what they had done.

I have had other similar experiences. I have had fellow alumni refuse to make contributions after lambasting me with what can only be called chauvinistic and even racist criticisms related to the changing demographics of the student population. When confronted on the substance of their comments, nearly all beat a hasty retreat. Seldom, however, was this followed by an acknowledgment of the inappropriateness of their comments or a contribution. Instead, I would likely be treated to a new litany of complaints dealing with minor administrative decisions such as campus parking, alumni magazine articles, honorary doctorates awarded, and the like. I would also likely hear complaints about the way the endowment portfolio was being mishandled.

Although I have tried over the years to respond to these criticisms, I have reached the conclusion that what irritates these alumni most is the fact that they don't seem to count as much as they feel is their due. Even those persons making racist and chauvinistic comments seem more irritated by the fact that their college has changed than by the race and gender of the new arrivals. It is the change, per se, that bothers them more than the nature of the change. As bizarre as it might be, I have concluded that most of these critics feel more comfortable complaining about race and gender than acknowledging that they feel ignored. The fact that I have seldom "won back" such critics with quite elegant arguments in defense of diversity, but have "won back" many by rejecting their views but stressing that they remain part of the institution and not forsake it, would support this conclusion. I often pointed out that when we were in school, certain older alumni looked upon us as different. We had also engaged in various forms of protest. Moreover, the present students were having a similar educational experience to ours and were responding in much the same way, going on to graduate school and careers in business and the professions. I also pointed out that whatever their backgrounds, the present students are as committed to the college as we were.

The question of who owns American higher education is not limited to turf battles between those within and those outside these institutions. Similar turf battles go on daily within the institutions themselves. To a large extent, these battles relate to the inherent strains that characterize the interlocked system of faculty and administration rights and responsibilities, noted earlier. These confrontations are normally articulated in terms of the previously described inclusiveness, curriculum, and employment issues.

Given the nature of internecine conflict, it is also not surprising that internal dissidents and critics are commonly the source of the most negative portraits of an institution's management principles and practices. Being insiders, they know best where the skeletons are and are in a position to publicize them, to the embarrassment of those whom they single out. What makes these criticisms so caustic is that they are generally liberally mixed with what might be called institutional sour grapes and all of the bitterness and anecdotal detail that serve to give their accounts a powerful aftertaste.

Other, more prosaic, factors feed into the proclivity to judge the management of higher education negatively. Higher education has undergone and is undergoing major structural changes. Whenever important institutions change, a high degree of uneasiness will often surface as criticism. In addition, higher education, because it continually evaluates and judges people, is by its very nature in the business of rewarding some and, unfortunately, disadvantaging others. It is not just a simple matter of acceptance and rejection of student applicants, though that clearly is a major issue, especially when dealing with the more prestigious and high-profile institutions. Higher education is engaged in an ongoing process of certification and evaluation in which only a minority flourish.

All of these factors lay the foundation for negativism. Like the other sources of discontent described earlier, however, these highly personal hurts do not provide a sound basis for formulating public critiques. On the other hand, nearly all of these experienced hurts are a direct result of management policies, decisions, and personnel. If there exists an acceptable rubric through which one can express one's negative feelings, it is likely to receive a fair amount of support. Complaining about poor management in general provides such a rubric. It normally doesn't matter that there is little or no evidence that such management practices are fiscally inefficient. In fact, it normally doesn't matter if there is a complete absence of real fiscal and management analysis.

Although it may seem convoluted and even frivolous, another source of negativism remains that, I believe, has served to feed the attacks on higher education. In fact, I would suggest that it has been the basis of many other criticisms noted herein, especially criticism from those on the political right. Simply put, higher education began to take itself too seriously. As a consequence, it became a threat to an important segment of the public that historically had been highly supportive and even protective of higher education.

I should stress that the chain of events that I am about to describe as producing this situation is quite speculative. Moreover, it was neither intended nor predicted. The process began, I would suggest, with critics lambasting higher education for not giving enough attention to educational outcomes. That is, educational institutions were criticized for overemphasizing educational inputs such as the quality of their faculty, physical resources, and the intelligence and potential of their students while giving little attention to what students actually learned. In response to such criticisms, greater emphasis was placed on ensuring that students absorbed more of what they were being taught. Ironically, a number of these critics soon realized that they were not eager for students to absorb everything, especially some of the more radical political theories to which they were exposed.

It is sometimes hard to remember but prior to the 1950s and 1960s, American higher education was not a source of general national concern. In the first place, most people did not go to college. In the second place, most of those who did go to college attended more as a rite de passage than anything else. Even for students expected to acquire specific skills, as in the case of those pursuing professional careers, college did not represent a hurdle to be surmounted so much as an experience to be absorbed. Whatever technical skills were necessary for certain professions would be acquired later in graduate school and through apprenticeships. Professors, for their part, weren't expected to take undergraduates that seriously either. Those teaching in private institutions tended to look upon most students as superficial, privileged young men and sometimes women who had little real interest in the life of the mind. This relationship was aptly reflected in the notion of the "gentleman's C–."[61] The situation wasn't that different even at most public institutions. The students may have been less privileged than those attending private institutions, but few were considered by the faculty to be kindred spirits.

Students for their part, reflecting the views of their parents and elders, generally looked upon faculty members as eccentric, otherworldly individuals pursuing esoteric, often personal interests. Few parents expected or desired their offspring to return home with the values and views of their professors. Professors were to profess and their children were to benefit by being exposed to such men of learning. In many ways, the prevailing parental attitude was analogous to that which governed their interest in having their children spend a year abroad visiting museums and places of historical importance. College education was meant more to be a broadening experience than a molding experience. An added benefit was the fact that college faculties neither demanded high salaries nor an expensive supervisory infrastructure. They went about their business pretty much on their own, demanding relatively little in financial support.[62]

Given this general laissez-faire attitude, there was little concern that progressive or left-leaning faculty would, or even could, corrupt students. It was understood that the values and goals of many faculty members were different than those of the students and their parents, but this was not an issue of concern. Faculty members didn't seem to be very interested in transforming their students, many of whom gave the impression of caring more about their future careers than about larger ideas. Even if faculty members had wanted to convert their students, their social position and lifestyle didn't provide a highly seductive platform from which to do so. Moreover, on campus a solid mix of more conservative faculty was always present to offset whatever radical ideas were presented. These conservative faculty members, furthermore, generally controlled most administrative positions.

This all started to change in the 1960s and 1970s, as various forces began to make faculty members more responsible for what their students were getting out of the college and university experience.[63] The 1960s were a period of ideological upheaval on most American campuses. The civil rights movement and the war in Vietnam played central roles in this upheaval, but there were also the follow-up to the Russian Sputnik success and John F. Kennedy's evangelical youth crusade. "Ask not what your country can do for you, but what you can do for your country" and "The torch has been passed to a new generation" were two catch phrases of the period, both from President Kennedy's inaugural address. Closer to home, there was also the Free Speech movement at the University of California at Berkeley and civil rights and antiwar protests on campuses around the country.

Whatever the exact mixture of causes, students began to demand more attention from their faculty, while faculty members began to take their responsibility toward their students more seriously. At the same time, to meet the need for a greater number of faculty members to teach the growing numbers of college students, faculty salaries raced ahead. In the late 1960s a starting assistant professor could earn the equivalent of what would today be $75,000 a year, which was approximately what beginning lawyers earned. The burgeoning student body, meanwhile, contained many more students from lower-income families. Taken together, this placed the faculty in a significantly more respectable financial and social role than had been the case just a decade or so earlier.

While this new mutual interest and respect covered a wide range of issues, it tended to focus primarily upon political and moral issues. Whereas before, faculty and students seemed content to allow each other to go their own ideological ways, there now seemed to be a concerted effort on the part of elements in both groups, though clearly not all, to bring members of the other group along.

While partisans of nearly all political persuasions were active during this period, the political left emerged as dominant. Ironically, while many, probably most, adults in nonacademic communities attributed the move to the left to the faculty, the emergence of the left was due more to student activism than to faculty efforts. During this period, I was a graduate student at what was considered to be one of the most left-leaning universities. I can report that while a number of faculty members at that time would have classified themselves on the left, the great majority were by temperament and inclination politically cautious, if not inactive. Moreover, on my campus, as on nearly ever campus, left-leaning faculty members were clearly outnumbered by nonleftist faculty.

What is clear is that as a result of the events of the '60s, many social observers, especially those with a more conservative bent, became quite critical of what they saw to be radicalism and even anti-Americanism in a majority of higher education institutions. Most of these attacks focused on the political, antiwar, and civil rights rhetoric and actions that emanated from the campuses. Other attacks, especially those that emerged later, targeted what was seen to be the underlying cause of these political outbreaks, namely, a degradation of education itself. Here, the criticism was aimed at the faculty members who had forsaken the classical curriculum in an attempt to satisfy the revolutionary demands of the '60s. While most of these attacks focused on curriculum issues, faculty and institutions were often generally taken to task for being irresponsible. In these attacks, pretty much everything was, and often still is, considered fair game. It is here that these political objectives intersect with the pervasive tendency described earlier of accusing higher education of fiscal irresponsibility.

I am sure that some politically vocal critics who also attack higher education for fiscal irresponsibility are subject to the same misconceptions as fiscal critics without political goals. At other times, however, the fiscal criticism coming from political critics seems somewhat duplicitous—a case of taking advantage of the situation. It sometimes appears that these critics believe that if it is easier to get people to condemn higher education for fiscal irresponsibility than for its ideological/political stand on issues, then they will employ fiscal criticisms. In these latter situations, political concerns serve to confuse the situation by promoting what is in reality a false account of the fiscal reality of higher education. Generally, more than the fiscal situation, however, comes under attack. The overall management of higher education is also taken to task. *It is this combined attack upon general management practices, cost increases, and ideological/political items that serves to generate such a devastating, if fundamentally flawed, critique of higher education.*

Does this mean that everything is marvelous about the way higher education has traditionally been managed or that political criticisms are illegitimate? The answer to both questions is clearly no. Neither political criticisms nor the issues of curricula, student demographics and numbers, and academic standards support the criticisms dealing with tenure, sabbaticals, research time, and faculty governance. The problems, and there are major problems, are due to other factors. Some of these factors relate to questions bearing on what types of education American institutions of higher education should offer. These questions are clearly related to the ideological and political concerns underlying the complaints of many critics. Moreover, these issues have direct fiscal and managerial implications. The most pressing fiscal and managerial problems presently confronting American higher education, however, have a different source. More specifically, they tend to be products of innovations and alterations that were introduced to correct the false difficulties detailed in this and the previous chapter. These innovations, which I label "false cures," are at the root of most fiscal and managerial problems presently confronting our institutions of higher education.

Put more concretely, the real problems have little to do with runaway costs in and of themselves, but rather with faulty innovations, often claimed to be market oriented, introduced to cut costs and increase income. Similarly, traditional higher education management principles and practices, including academic tenure, sabbatical leaves, and faculty governance, are not the source of major difficulties, but the actions taken to circumvent and change these policies and practices—again, often justified on supposed market principles—have created real havoc.

As destructive as these various cures have been—and we shall look at both the cures and their impact shortly—they have caused correlative damage by fostering false accusations and thereby hindering us from confronting the real problems. They have had another negative impact. By framing themselves in the rhetoric of the market, they have made the market an anathema to many, especially many faculty members, within higher education. The reality is that market principles can often be applied successfully in dealing with existing fiscal problems in higher education. Before we can confront these real problems and explore various possible solutions, however, we need to understand these faulty cures.

Part II

The Pitfalls of Faulty Economic Cures

5

∾

Cutting Costs
and Raising Revenues

The purpose of this chapter is to explore some of the practices that various institutions have put in place to stop, or minimally control, what they assumed to be runaway costs. The two most obvious ways to do this would be to cut costs and to raise new revenues.[64] While most institutions have tried to do both, it shouldn't surprise anyone familiar with the way most organizations function that the greater effort has gone into raising revenues. It is part of the empire-building syndrome in which growth nearly always seems to be preferred over cutbacks. Nevertheless, we will begin with some of the more common cost-cutting procedures in higher education.

The simplest and most straightforward option available to most academic administrations would be to eliminate or reduce specific programs. The problem is that programs not only cost money, they also generate revenues. What complicates matters even more is the fact that programs are seldom funded in isolation from other programs. This makes it often very difficult to allocate costs precisely. The same problem arises when it comes to determining the revenues earned by a particular program. There is often a synergism between programs, in which an apparently uneconomical program or academic unit might be essential to the operation of a profitable program.

A simple example of this could be the relationship between a costly economic department with few majors and a large, fairly inexpensive—it relies heavily on adjunct teachers—accounting department with many majors. In short, a small program that apparently costs more than it earns may be essential for a much larger program that ostensibly earns more than it costs. What further complicates all of this is the fact that unlike the case just noted, the connection may not be apparent. Education majors, for example, may be required to take a particular history or political science course for their state certification.

The most obvious way to avoid such problems in eliminating programs would be to obtain the advice of those most knowledgeable about such requirements and cross-departmental/program dependencies. Unfortunately, this approach is fraught with its own difficulties. To begin with, even those responsible for managing a given program may be ignorant of the full extent of the various interdependencies that might exist. And even if they are aware of these interdependencies, they seldom are capable of making any sort of rational economic judgments regarding the consequence of eliminating one or another element and establishing alternatives. Equally troubling is the fact that those best able to shed some light on the existent economic interconnections and implications also tend to be those with the most self-interest in these programs. As such, they are very unlikely to share information that is apt to lead to cuts in these programs.

So what have most administrators done?

Probably the most common strategy pursued by academic administrators seeking ways to cut programs is the favored academic strategy for dealing with any situation, namely, establishing a committee. Considering that most such committees generally fail to recommend any sort of decisive action, this is in many ways a very sound strategy. By establishing a committee, the administration can claim to be dealing with the issue while at the same time protecting itself from having to actually do anything. As we shall see, considering the options, this is often the best strategy to follow. It is not, however, a painless option. For one thing, such committees are costly. They are generally made up of a good number of well-paid administrators and faculty members. They tend to meet fairly often and for numerous weeks. In short, while the institution rarely bothers to calculate what such committees cost, let alone bill itself for the time spent by all in these meetings, the sum is not inconsequential.

Faculty and administrative hours represent only part of the institutional costs of such committees. Even when such committees fail to generate any action plans or even formal recommendations, their deliberations alone often serve to produce institutional controversies. In part, these controversies grow directly out of the issues under review and the fact that different people have different self-interests. The ad hoc committee process, however, generally serves to heighten these controversies since there are always grounds for objecting to the way such committees are established and staffed. Normally, some degree of confidentiality governs committee discussions, which, while serving to avoid some conflicts, also serves to exacerbate institutional paranoia.

Even assuming that such committees seldom are able to come to closure, their cost might be supportable if their rare recommendations were generally sound. Unfortunately, even when such committees do come to closure, their recommendations tend to reflect political objectives more than either academic or economic objectives. More specifically, the programs that most often tend to be recommended for elimination or cutbacks are not necessarily, or even normally, academically questionable or economically costly programs, but those with fewer or weaker institutional allies and supporters. This is not only unfair, but also wrongheaded.

Even when a politically weak, targeted program or department has serious academic deficiencies, eliminating or cutting back resources may be the worst strategy to follow, especially when the program is essential to a strong overall academic program. On the other hand, politically strong, academically questionable programs are generally able not only to deflect attacks upon them, but to use such attacks as opportunities to rally their supporters and acquire additional resources. Other politically strong departments, including academically sound departments, may also use such review processes to acquire more resources than may be legitimately merited. The fact is that a department or program defined as strong or weak at any particular moment may be so designated at least partially because of the past support it has received rather than from any inherent strength or weakness.

Even more troubling than decisions that grow out of political strengths and weaknesses rather than academic and institutional needs are those that reflect personal and/or ideological biases. While such decisions are sometimes the product of committees, they are more often made unilaterally by administrators.[65] Some ideologically biased decisions, such as the attacks in the early 1990s on the sociology departments at Washington University and Yale by top administrators, have received national attention.[66] More common and less noted, however, are those based on personal biases. And no program or department is immune. A few years ago, a president at one of the CUNY colleges, in expectation of retrenchment, recommended eliminating the English department because the department had shown itself "uncooperative." In most cases, such recommendations are not acted upon, but they are, nevertheless, disruptive.

The fact that reorganization recommendations of the sorts noted herein generally prove to be counterproductive does not negate the fact that a number of programs probably deserve to be cut or minimally reduced while many more do not perform up to the standards that they should. The goal in most cases, however, should be to find ways to get such programs and departments functioning at the appropriate level. The situation reminds me of an old Talmudic story in which Rabbi Akiba prays that G-d remove from the earth all wicked people. His wife tells him that it is wrong to pray for the death of anyone, even the wicked. What he should pray for is the removal of wickedness. Similarly, while eliminating weak programs may generate some short-term benefits, it's better to find ways of improving such programs.[67]

The nonsense generated from broad efforts to cut programs was dramatically revealed in a report of the City University of New York, officially titled

The Chancellor's Advisory Committee on Academic Program Planning, but commonly called the *Goldstein Report* after the committee's chair. The committee was appointed by the past chancellor of the City University of New York in March of 1992 and delivered its report in December of the same year.[68] Under pressure from state legislators to cut costs and increase efficiency, Chancellor Reynolds established a committee under the chairmanship of Leon Goldstein, who was then the president of one of the community colleges in the CUNY system. The committee was charged with recommending ways to cut costs. After meeting for approximately a year, it recommended that a wide range of programs be eliminated on particular campuses and that students interested in pursuing such programs do so by taking the required courses at other campuses. Ostensibly, by eliminating "duplicate" programs the university could save money.

Unfortunately, the report failed to take into consideration numerous things. It failed to account for the costs involved in traveling from campus to campus, the way different programs fitted together on particular campuses, different scheduling practices, the existing and projected economies of scale of the various programs, or, for that matter, any of the actual academic and economic implications of its recommendations. Fortunately, the report generated sufficient opposition that it was shelved. Nevertheless, it served to disrupt the entire university for over a year, forcing faculty and administrators throughout the system to expend hours of time and energy in responding to its array of false assumptions, conclusions, and recommendations.

Another way to save money is to attempt to eliminate or reduce specific staff benefits.

Some of the most common targets for such cutbacks are, not surprisingly, the same benefits and practices decried in chapters 1 and 3, namely, tenure, sabbatical leaves, faculty research, and "light" teaching loads. Individual administrators have focused on a wide range of other practices peculiar to particular institutions. What these reduction efforts generally have in common is that they prove to be counterproductive. Rather than saving money or increasing efficiency, they have just the opposite effect.

One example from the City University of New York with which I am personally familiar might help to illustrate the type of unanticipated complications that such actions often produce. This example revolves around changes in what is called the university's *Multiple Position* policy, which governs the types of employment that faculty members are allowed to pursue in addition to their normal teaching assignments.

For as long as I can remember, and I have been at CUNY for over thirty years, every faculty member has been required to fill out a form each semester indicating what additional paid and unpaid employment he or she had for the semester. The rules for many years limited such employment to the equivalent of one day's additional work per week. The faculty member would fill out these forms, which had to be approved first by the department chair, then the dean, and so on. Most faculty had little or no additional employment, particularly little to no additional *paid* employment. A few faculty members, usually in the sciences or economics, reported some paid consulting work. In the system as a whole, however, the largest reported sources of additional employment were adjunct salaries received for teaching additional courses and income received through research grants. In the great majority of cases, the additional course and the grant were offered and administered by the college where the faculty member was employed.

In the mid-1990s someone at the central office apparently became disturbed by the fact that certain faculty members were increasing their future pension payments, creating modest additional costs to the university, by teaching a number of additional courses during their last years before retiring. By teaching the extra courses, they increased their overall salary for the final years, which was used to calculate their pensions. It should be noted that the number of people doing this was extremely small, since the opportunity to increase one's pension in this way was limited to a small percentage of older faculty members who had selected a particular retirement plan. Nevertheless, in classic bureaucratic style, this "discovery" led to a new policy of banning any additional paid employment when such employment was paid through the university.

It is probable that this policy change served to save a few dollars on a few pensions.[69] Not many, however, because, as noted, only a small minority of the faculty was involved. The unanticipated costs of this policy change, however, were enormous. For one thing, as soon as faculty members realized that they couldn't pay themselves anything during the academic years from a grant run through the university, those who could quickly moved their grants to other institutions. As a result, the university lost the overhead on these grants. Similarly, faculty members who had been willing to take on a heavy normal teaching load in order to be assigned an extra overload course for which they could be paid, declined to continue with the heavier than normal teaching loads they had been carrying.[70] Replacing such faculty with part-time adjuncts consequently not only didn't save money, but actually cost money since there were additional courses to cover. The replacement faculty, moreover, tended to be less experienced and qualified than the regular faculty that had been replaced.

Other simpler, more straightforward strategies that some institutions have attempted to implement include a general increase in teaching loads and an increase in class size. Unfortunately, these tactics seldom produce their desired objectives. It is very difficult to force faculty members to do anything they believe to be wrong or unfair, since there is no extensive supervisory infrastructure in place to monitor and enforce administrative injunctions. It is quite easy for any faculty member to sabotage any effort to increase the number of students in his or her class by assigning more work and otherwise presenting a highly demanding profile during the first few classes of a semester. Such actions can very quickly reduce the number of students in a given class. This response can also be used to reduce class size in general so that faculty members forced to teach additional classes may end up actually teaching fewer students in total than they initially taught in less classes.

Many, if not most, administrators recognize the difficulty they confront in attempting to coerce faculty members to increase their workloads. Some, if not all, consequently have elected to circumvent the problem by simply replacing full-time faculty with part-time faculty. Given that a course taught by a part-time faculty person normally costs significantly less than half and sometimes as little as a tenth of that taught by a full-time faculty person, this strikes many administrators as an attractive option. Financially, it is, at least in the short run. The education produced, however, is clearly not of the same quality. Such lowering of quality in what has become a very competitive market, more often than not, leads to a drop in enrollment and an eventual loss of income.[71]

Academic administrations have attempted to implement other procedures in an attempt to cut costs, or at least appear to be attempting to do so. One such procedure that re-emerges at regular intervals on some campuses entails closer management and stricter allocation of classrooms. If one examines the class schedule of nearly any institution of higher education, one will see that classroom facilities are not used equally throughout the day, week, or year. Given the prevalent semester/quarter schedules of nearly all institutions of higher learning, coupled with a wide range of holidays, classes are scheduled during some weeks and not others. During those weeks when classes are held, moreover, they tend to be scheduled more on some days than others and during some hours more than others.

Some administrators argue that a more even distribution of classes would be more economically efficient. This argument rests heavily on assumptions that a more balanced schedule will require fewer facilities in the long run. Others argue that it will attract more *customers*. This latter argument will be commented upon only briefly now, since it isn't a cost-saving argument but rather an income-raising argument. When it is pointed out that the cost of facilities is determined more by the size of the facilities rather than their use, the argument is made that a more balanced use allows for greater use, which converts into less need for additional facilities and hence future savings.

While there is clearly some merit to this argument for institutions that are experiencing a shortage of space and can elect either to use their present space more efficiently or build new space, the argument also has major flaws. Spreading out the use of most facilities, in and of itself, actually increases rather than reduces costs. One clear example of this is the additional costs entailed by keeping a building heated or cooled on days when it would otherwise be closed. Normally, there are also additional maintenance staff costs. Similarly, while a more distributed schedule may attract new students, it can also serve to rebuff them. The skewed schedules that are common to most institutions have evolved over a number of years and in most cases they reflect the needs and demands not only of faculty, but also of students.

At Queens College, for example, there tends to be a lower number of classes on Friday than on Monday through Thursday. A number of different administrations, claiming that this is costly and merely reflects the faculty's desire for long weekends, have attempted to schedule more Friday classes. In fact, the lopsided schedule has little to nothing to do with faculty desires for longer weekends, as evidenced by the fact that Monday is the busiest day of the week. (This is not to deny that many faculty members prefer to have Friday free, but most of them use this time to pursue their own research.) It is due rather to student preferences related to their job schedules and to the fact that the college has a high proportion of Orthodox Jewish students. Given this situation, it is not surprising that most faculty members regard administrative crusades to increase the number of Friday classes as nothing more than a form of administrative harassment, due to administrators' irritation that they have to come in on Fridays while many faculty members are free to work at home.

One other cost-cutting talisman deserves to be mentioned: technology, especially the greater use of computers and distance learning. Whereas elimination and reduction of programs, reduced benefits, increased teaching loads, greater reliance on part-time teachers, and more efficient use of space have been around for a while, the possibility of saving money through a greater use of technology is relatively recent. While the jury is still out on this one, the evidence so far isn't very promising. It is not that modern technology is incapable of servicing great numbers of people with all sorts of information relatively inexpensively. It is. It is just that most educators see such technology as providing added educational capabilities to their curriculum rather than as a substitute for what is presently offered. For most institutions, consequently, technology has so far been an added expense, not a money-saver. Whether it might become a money-saver is another issue that cannot be resolved without examining the broader issues of what should constitute a higher education and how it can be packaged. I think it is fair to say, however, that technology as a cost saver is presently only a dream, not a reality.

While the discussion presented here reveals that these various strategies, even when well-intentioned, are both conceptually and practically flawed, I haven't fully conveyed the damage commonly generated by such cost-cutting strategies. Not only do they seldom save money, but in fact, they often end up increasing costs. They also frequently serve to undermine the very heart and soul of the institution where they are implemented. No institution, not even the most well-endowed educational institution, can survive while oblivious to its economic reality. Cost-saving discussions, however, must be grounded in broader concerns dealing with the educational goals of the institution. The same can be said for economic discussions that focus on efforts to increase revenues.

While nearly all administrators minimally have to pay lip service to controlling costs, most would much prefer to resolve their economic problems by increasing revenues. Administrators of every type would rather expand their empire than diminish it. Unfortunately, academic administrators tend to be no more successful at increasing revenues that they are in reducing costs. On the other hand, they do try in all sorts of ways. Some of their most common strategies include:

increasing tuition income;
obtaining more external research grants;
raising the level of private and foundation gifts;
developing economically beneficial ties with business; and
instituting new, profitable academic and/or auxiliary programs.

One of the drawbacks to increasing tuition was noted earlier. It was pointed out that while tuition increases do generate some additional income, a large proportion of any theoretical increase is offset by increases in scholarships and other forms of financial support. Among the elite private institutions that maintain an aid-blind acceptance policy, financial aid commonly ranges from 25 percent to 50 percent of tuition revenue.[72] In the case of many public institutions where tuition formerly played a minor role in the overall finances of the institution, increases in tuition and financial aid have also generated a mammoth increase in support staff to process these monies. In most cases, some net increase in income remains, but nothing like the sums that the raw figures would suggest.

Whatever extra income is generated by tuition increases, there are also offsetting costs to keep in mind. The largest of these is the stress and strain placed upon students and their families. With the rise of tuition costs, many students are obliged to work longer hours at nonacademic jobs. When I first came to Queens College in the '60s, few day students worked more than five hours a week. Evening students, who generally did not take a full academic course load, worked between twenty and forty hours a week. Today, with tuition and fees approaching $4,000 a year, day students work on average over twenty hours a week and most evening students hold down full-time jobs and then often work additional hours. There is no way that these obligations can fail to negatively influence students' academic work. As a result, fewer students graduate and those who do take longer to do so. This is costly not only to the students involved but also to the institution, since more courses have to be repeated and more students are lost.

One could argue, which I personally do all the time, that the resources invested in students who do not graduate are not wasted. On the other hand, there is growing evidence that from a societal perspective, a person's over-all financial and social rewards increase with his or her years of education.[73] While the cost of a single year of college for four different individuals may cost approximately the same as four years of college for one individual, the single individual with four years of college will generate greater additional earnings and tax revenues than the four individuals with one year of college will do collectively. Perhaps more important, from an educational perspective, the four-year experience will also generate greater knowledge gains. Admittedly, there are advantages in providing access to higher education to greater numbers of people. There is something fundamentally wrong, however, with a system that finances such access through increased tuition costs that force students to invest more of their time and energy in external employment. Such employment often prevents students from satisfactorily fulfilling their academic obligations and ends with their forced or voluntary abandonment of educational goals. However one calculates the cost, there is significant waste in an educational system that makes it difficult if not impossible for a large percentage of its students to succeed. And this has been and is one of the by-products of tuition inflation, whatever additional revenue such increases may have produced.

The situation described here, while not unique to public institutions, is probably more characteristic of such institutions than of private institutions, especially the more prestigious private ones that pride themselves on providing an adequate financial package for those students needing financial support. Even in the private sector, however, increases in tuition have their costs. Whereas thirty years ago financial support generally meant a scholarship, such financial support today entails a financial mix of loans, jobs, and scholarships. Moreover, in recent years there has been a sizable shift in the mix, with students being expected to work more hours and to borrow more money than was the case even ten years ago.

Few scholarship students at private institutions are expected to put in the twenty-plus hours per week that many students at public institutions work, but large numbers of them are working more hours than their academic schedules can reasonably bear. Perhaps more destructive in the long run, however, is the debt that many of these students are forced to assume. It is becoming common for students to complete their undergraduate education owing tens of thousands of dollars. Many students complete their graduate education with loans approaching and even surpassing $100,000. Some, unwilling to take on such debt, drop out. Others are forced to pursue careers for purely financial reasons. In both cases, society as a whole is often the loser.

After tuition increases, perhaps the most commonly pursued pot of gold has been and remains external research grants. These grants have historically been sought primarily by large research institutions and smaller elite colleges. Both types of institutions claim that their faculty is deeply engaged in research and scholarship and use this fact to justify their faculty's rather modest teaching load. More recently, however, nearly everyone has joined the chase. They have been encouraged not only by the granting agencies and foundations that have sought to spread their wealth around more broadly, but also by the availability of more funds directed at issues and programs more pertinent to the mission of comprehensive, less elite educational institutions.[74]

Research grants, regardless of their origin or stated objectives, offer all sorts of economic rewards. Not only can they be used to fund part or all of participating faculty salaries, a wide range of expensive equipment, travel, support staff, and other directly accountable items, but they normally also come with what is called institutional overhead, which the institution can use to augment its general activities. Historically, such overhead often ran 85 percent and higher than the direct costs entailed in the grant, providing a very nice reward to the institutions capable of procuring them.

Unfortunately, even these precious jewels are not quite as valuable as they appear, or as they once might have been. To begin with, most granting institutions have in recent years dramatically cut back on the general overhead that they are willing to pay. Many grants now come with overheads as low as 10 percent or less. While one might argue that 10 percent is better than nothing, in truth it is often worth less than nothing since grants always generate some costs, usually in excess of 10 percent of the total award. I have not met a grant officer yet who would not admit that grants with an overhead of 10 percent or less actually cost the institution money.

There are other unanticipated costs. It is always nice when an external institution is willing to absorb the cost of a faculty member's salary, especially when it is a big salary. They aren't doing it for nothing, however. When a faculty member receives a grant that buys out his or her time, he or she is no longer available to fulfill the teaching and other responsibilities previously assigned. Admittedly, the host institution can use the money received from the grant to hire a replacement. Moreover, it can often do so for less money than it received from the grant. On the other hand, if the institution elects to hire a less-expensive adjunct faculty member, the quality of the instruction that the students receive is likely to be of a lower quality. An added problem is that any replacement faculty also needs space and, minimally, some secretarial and administrative support. None of these things are free. In fact, if the replacement hired is a full-time person, even one making significantly less than the grant-winner, there is likely to be very little left over from the buy-out money once all the support costs have been paid.

Much the same situation holds for other grant funds. It is always exciting when a grant allows an institution to purchase sought-after equipment, but such equipment has to be maintained and serviced. Sometimes a grant will provide partial if not full funding for such maintenance during the life of the grant, but even in these cases the host institution ends up paying the costs when the grant period ends.

In addition, there are the very real costs of administering a grant, as noted earlier. Nearly every granting source requires that the institution receiving the grant account for the way the money is spent. There are also requests for progress reports and other types of information. Someone has to prepare these documents and this person is seldom a volunteer. Here, I can't help but relate what is perhaps an apocryphal account of a program for musically gifted students from deprived backgrounds. It cost practically 75 percent of the total funds awarded just to find and select a cohort of students that would meet the participation guidelines. Another 10 percent was spent in documenting the program, leaving less than 15 percent for the program itself. Since the actual program had been budgeted at 60 percent of the grant, the host institution was forced to absorb the 45-percent difference.

There are normally other institutional costs involved in obtaining grants. The most common relate to "matching costs." Put quite simply, nearly all granting sources require that the institution seeking external support match external funds with its own funds. There are, admittedly, a number of ways that these figures can be fudged. An institution can claim that a particular faculty member will dedicate a third of his or her time to a particular project and then build in a third of this faculty member's salary plus fringe benefits as its match. In actuality the faculty member may put in no more than 10 percent of his or her time on the project. Even when the time is reported accurately, the costs tend to be inflated since the faculty member is likely to be replaced with a much cheaper adjunct instructor.

There are also facility and administrative costs that can be built in, which are costs that would have to be met even without the grant. These can include charges for office space, telephones, and the like. With all of these gambits, however, real costs are still generated. When it comes to grants, the days of getting something for nothing are gone.

Despite all of these drawbacks, grants and contracts have provided significant funding for numerous higher education institutions during the last few decades, particularly in the physical sciences. The situation clearly seems to have changed, however, as of late. To give two illustrations of this, during the last few years, a few educational institutions have attempted to get a better handle on where their money came from and where it went. The University of Rhode Island received a fair amount of press for its efforts.[75] What was particularly interesting about its analysis was that it discovered that the physical sciences, with their greater proportion of grants and contracts, rather than supporting the humanities and social sciences, were actually being subsidized by the humanities and social sciences. Put slightly differently, tuition income, rather than research grant money, was being used to subsidize

research. My own analysis of the situation at Queens College and some other
units of the City University of New York revealed a similar pattern.

In an effort to increase grants and contracts, the past chancellor, Ann
Reynolds, greatly enhanced the central office of the university's research
foundation. To fund this operation, what amounted to a 10 percent tax was
imposed on all grants. Unfortunately, this necessitated diverting overhead
from the better-funded grants to cover grants with little or no overhead. The
end result has been that during the last few years, as total grants at Queens
College have increased, the amount of money available to support college
activities has actually decreased. Where, for example, $5,000,000 in grants in
the past might have generated $1,000,000 in overhead, today that amount is
likely to generate less than $200,000. And, it should be noted, this does not
take into account a significant proportion of the college's costs in obtaining
and managing grant money, which are absorbed into the college's general
budget. As a result, it is questionable whether there has been any net gain,
despite a respectable gain in gross receipts.

Educational administrators have been aware of the illness, if not the death,
of their research-grant golden goose for some time. In an attempt to replace
this source of income, a growing number of educational institutions have
turned more aggressively toward wealthy individuals and the private sector,
seeking donations and attempting to establish joint ventures of varying sorts.
These ventures include establishing tailor-made courses, doing contract
research, and engaging in joint community ventures. For the business community these programs offer the possibility of not only obtaining desired
products at a comparatively cheap price, but also the possibility of enhancing its own image as a charitable and community-sensitive organization.

While a number of educational institutions have generated a resource
stream from these activities, there have been noteworthy costs. To begin with,
as with research projects, these activities commonly provide a greater drain
on institutional resources than expected. As a result, the income generated by
these activities is seldom as much as initially projected; this is not surprising
since the institution's business partners in these ventures are not prone to part
with their money easily. Moreover, these activities, being explicitly more
market-orientated, are often criticized as alien to the institution's basic academic mission, causing a degree of campus dissension and confusion.

Of all the various types of external funds available to an educational institution, gifts and donations would appear to be the safest. When such gifts
and donations are given as unrestricted gifts, this is true. All that is normally
required is some form of suitable recognition and perhaps a favor or two: a
questionable admission for a grandson, an honorary degree, or a shiny
plaque on a room or building. Large gifts and donations, however, often
come with serious restrictions. Donors may seek to exercise unacceptable
control over faculty appointments and/or curriculum, causing a good deal of

institutional distress.[76] The conditions attached to some gifts, however, can also prove to be an economic poison pill. More than one institution has been the proud recipient of a valuable art or literary collection, for example, only to discover that the maintenance and upkeep of the collection was terribly expensive. Other institutions have happily established endowed academic chairs, only to discover that their own costs in providing space, support staff, travel, telephone, postage, and administrative support far exceed what they had anticipated. Unfortunately, even when top administrators know that such gifts will actually cost the institution significant amounts of money, they commonly accepted them. Such gifts allow the administrators to claim success in raising funds for their institution even when, in fact, all that they are doing is generating additional long-term costs.[77]

While some administrators have looked outward in search of potentially economically beneficial new programs, other administrators have favored going it on their own. The guiding principle in these cases is to attempt to discover an untapped academic market that can be profitably exploited. It may be an unmet demand for health-care providers, math teachers, or other skilled workers, on the one hand, or working mothers, foreign students, or municipal workers desiring an academic program better structured to meet both their academic and lifestyle needs. Here again, the promise generally proves more economically appealing than the reality. The demand is seldom as great as anticipated while the costs of offering the program generally prove greater.

In some cases, such as the various health-care programs, including one initiated under CUNY Chancellor Reynolds at Lehman College in the early '90s, the market for workers can dissipate just as students begin to graduate. In the case of various weekend and summer programs, the problem has often been the lack of a sufficient number of students to make the program economically feasible. What complicates matters is that these difficulties are often not obvious initially. In the case of a weekend college, for example, an initial survey may reveal that there are potentially 5,000 students for such a program, which can function profitably with only 3,000 students. What the survey fails to reveal, however, is that only 1,000 students are interested in pursuing the handful of majors and academic programs to be offered in the weekend college. Moreover, whereas the survey indicated that regular faculty would staff the weekend college, the budget only provides funds for adjunct replacements.

There can be other drawbacks to such programs. Whether economically feasible or not, these types of programs, whether they are labor-force initiatives or are marketed toward nontraditional students, are often perceived as downgrading the overall academic quality of the institution. This is particularly a problem when they originate within an institution that is self-defined as a liberal arts and sciences, research, or simply academic institution. When this occurs, significant numbers of faculty members, students, and alumni are apt to feel that their college has lost its direction and even its intellectual integrity. In the case of alumni, such feelings can and often do transform themselves into a degree of detachment and a reduction in financial support.

Attempting to satisfy student or, as some might say, *customer demands* is equally perilous. The problem is that students, especially those coming from educationally limited backgrounds, are generally not the best persons to make such decisions. Giving the customer what he or she wants in this particular case may prove to be worthless, or minimally worth less than the student/customer expected. From an institutional perspective it could be argued cynically that it really doesn't matter as long as students enroll and pay their bills. It does matter, however, even from a purely financial position because sooner or later, usually sooner, the customers will discover the true value of the program and demand will dry up. More to the point, it will normally dry up long before the start-up costs of the program have been recouped, leaving the institution with a net deficit.

As a result of all of the unintended and unanticipated negative repercussions that auxiliary programs are apt to generate, the long-term financial benefits are debatable at best. Unfortunately, this often doesn't matter to the new breed of administrators most eager to launch such programs. It doesn't matter because like the highly mobile new administrators flourishing in all sorts of organizations, the name of the game isn't long-term economic gains, but instead short-term gains or, even better, the appearance of potential gains. This is due to the fact that a good number of these administrators are much more interested in enhancing their own resumes rather than strengthening the institutions they have been entrusted to lead. This problem, however, revolves more around the issue of changes and proposed cures of institutional management, to be dealt with in the next chapter.

Are we to conclude from this that there are no ways in which costs of higher education can be reduced or its revenues increased? As we will see in subsequent chapters, both cost reductions and revenue enhancement are possible. Neither, however, can be accomplished in a significant way or for the long haul by cutting here and patching on there. Greater economic efficiency can only be achieved by altering and improving the fundamental procedures governing the way funds are procured and allocated. It also requires coordinating these decisions with the long-term educational goals of the institution. Ironically, this means analyzing the institution in terms of its numerous real internal and external markets. By falsely framing the failed attempts at top-down financial management as market-based initiatives, the faulty cures described in this chapter have not only generated additional costs, but have also served to sour many people on the very possibility of engaging in serious financial management. In the language of the title of this book, the faulty uses of market values have not only created pitfalls, but have also served to undermine the promise of market values.

6

~

Expanding
Academic Administration

As accusations of fiscal mismanagement tend to evolve into accusations of general administrative mismanagement, so efforts to effect fiscal changes tend to evolve into efforts to fundamentally alter administrative structures. Such has been the case with higher education, where what can only be called an administrative revolution has been and is in process. This revolution has been so rapid, profound, and widespread that it has become more and more difficult even to describe what academic administration is anymore.

In presenting the many criticisms leveled at academic administrations in earlier chapters, I implicitly accepted what might be called the traditional model of such administrations, namely, an administration that was largely local, long term, traditional, and limited in size and authority. While such a definition is clearly not an accurate description of what all academic administrations have historically been, it is even less an accurate description of what a growing number of academic administrations have become. It is, nevertheless, a useful characterization for understanding and evaluating the various administrative and organizational changes that have been recommended and institutionalized in recent years.

To a large extent, these changes have been generated by the criticism of traditional administrative principles and practices detailed in chapter 3: namely, that academic administrations are too local and inbred, too entrenched, too traditional in how they do things, too tolerant of faculty actions, insufficiently accountable, and, most important, weak and ineffective. To correct this situation, a number of senior administrators and governing boards have sought to do some of the following things: (1) recruit new leadership from outside the institution; (2) increase the turnover of senior management; (3) grant administrative leadership more powers vis-à-vis the faculty; (4) increase the overall strength of the administration by funding significant administrative growth[78] and more attractive administrative salaries; and (5) foster greater administrative centralization. What have these efforts produced?

Not surprisingly, one thing they clearly have produced has been larger, better paid, more powerful, more transient, more centralized, and less homegrown administrations. Whether these administrations have been any more efficient or productive than former administrations is an entirely different question. For the most part, the evidence would indicate that they haven't. In fact, analysis reveals that each of these changes has not only increased costs but has also been counterproductive in its impact on the host institutions where it has been implemented. What makes this situation more troubling is the fact that even fairly superficial reflection reveals that such results should have been expected. Let's take a closer look at each.

What happens when leadership is imported from outside? The proponents of this strategy generally argue that one acquires new blood, new energy, and new ideas. Leaders from outside aren't wedded to the old ways of doing things. They are in a better position to change things around rapidly. All of this might be true, but is it helpful? If things are presently in horrendous shape, the potential rewards might be worth the predictable risks, but if things are not in horrendous shape, it is unlikely that the gains will outweigh the losses.

It is questionable whether massive importation of external leadership will produce more gains than losses even when things are pretty bad. A little external blood might help, but a full infusion is as likely to kill the patient as to help. When the patient is healthy or simply has a cold, such infusions are likely to be needless, foolish, and even dangerous. Here it is only necessary to list some of the more likely costs of such a strategy.

Recruiting externally always proves to be significantly more expensive than promoting from within. First, there is the cost of the search and recruitment process itself. An external search requires not only extensive advertisements but, for senior-level appointments, usually a professional recruitment (i.e., "headhunting") firm. There are significant travel, hotel, and entertainment costs in not only bringing candidates to the college or university, but also in sending college delegates and delegations to other campuses. Add on telephone and secretarial costs and the total seldom comes to less than the annual salary of a solid associate professor.

Having recruited a suitable and desirable candidate, it becomes necessary to negotiate an acceptable salary. While it is also necessary to negotiate a salary with a new administrator selected internally, it nearly always costs more to bring someone in from outside.[79] There are moving and often housing costs as well. When all of these sums are added up, the new appointee commonly demands considerably more than his or her predecessor received. In contrast, for someone hired within, it is usually sufficient to offer approximately the same salary and benefits as the predecessor received. Another cost factor normally comes into play. An insider is already on salary. It may, of course, be necessary to hire a replacement for this person, but, on the other hand, it may not.

This whole situation becomes further complicated by the fact that it is normal procedure to grant senior administrators faculty status when they are appointed. In fact, senior administrators are nearly always given tenure in one or another academic department as a form of job security. This means that when senior administrators are replaced, they often don't go off the payroll but rather remain on the payroll in another capacity. In most cases, their academic salary is less, but it still tends to be higher than that of most faculty members.[80] Unfortunately, these individuals have often not taught for many years and are seldom worth an assistant professor's salary, let alone that of a distinguished professor. While these ex-administrators' salaries are allocated to instructional costs, they are really hidden administrative costs.

One of the advantages of selecting a senior administrator internally is that it does not entail a new tenured professorial appointment. Moreover, when an administrator seeks to step down, or when it is decided to replace him or her, this person can normally return to his or her old academic position. He or she may be somewhat out of touch with what is going on in the field, but it is much easier to return to an academic department to which one previously belonged than to enter a completely new department. In addition, if the person was selected internally, he or she was probably a valued and respected member of the community. Returning to the community, providing there were no major confrontations or disputes in the interim, is, as a consequence, likely to be harmonious. The situation will probably be very different for someone who has never previously been a colleague and has little or no social capital in reserve.

There are other drawbacks to bringing in external leaders. They lack institutional memory. While this may be seen as advantageous in situations where there is a strong desire to change, ignorance, even in the form of being oblivious of institutional memories, seldom proves to be an asset. Institutional memories not only enable one to avoid all sorts of traps and quagmires, but also help one to locate buried treasures and untapped reserves. Trying to navigate one's way through the potentially treacherous terrain of academia without such knowledge is somewhat foolhardy. Admittedly, it is not necessary for everyone in an academic administration to know where all the traps and reserves are buried. It is required, however, that someone knows.

When the fad for outside leaders began in the 1980s (my own best estimate of the time), this problem was minimal because there were enough old-timers with highly developed institutional memories. Today, unfortunately, many institutions are led by administrators who collectively have little to no institutional memory. I have seen this process unfold at my own institution. From the mid-'60s to the early '90s, with the exception of the president, nearly all senior administrators were internal appointments. In 1991, senior administrators averaged over twenty years at the college. In 1998, in a senior administration composed of approximately twelve persons, perhaps three had been at the college for three or more years. Even including two acting appointments of individuals who had been at the college for many years, the average for all administrators was less than five years.

Institutional memories are not the only thing lost with the transition to externally recruited administrators. There is also a significant loss of institutional loyalties. It is not that, as human beings, this new breed of administrators is inherently less loyal. Strictly speaking, the issue is not even that the administrators were externally recruited. The problem is that the system has changed. Most of the new administrators assume that if they want to pursue an administrative career, they should expect to move on to another institution within a few years. This type of professional mobility requires that they maintain an extensive network of friends, colleagues, and contacts beyond their present institution. They not only have to maintain their personal relationships, but also must follow what is happening at other institutions. This requires attending a greater number of professional meetings and more extensive travel than their predecessors, as well as making a certain adjustment in their own priorities. Their present institution can't command the fealty or allegiance that was expected from senior administrators in the past.

The constant attention to what is going on outside the institution is related to the other side of this practice of seeking external leadership, namely, the increased turnover of academic administrators. The fact that more and more institutions are recruiting externally means that more and more administrators are lured away from their present jobs, forcing their own institutions to repeat the practice in a game of musical chairs. This constant turnover serves to exacerbate the loss of both institutional memories and institutional loyalties. There are other drawbacks. Rather than committing themselves to institutional issues, itinerant administrators from this new breed commonly focus on building their own resumes in preparation for their next move. And they don't have a lot of time because the tenure of senior administrators is presently estimated at approximately four to five years.

How does one build a résumé? The primary task is to accumulate an impressive list of new initiatives and accomplishments. Nurturing existing programs and long-range planning don't have the same pizzazz. With apologies for any offense it might cause, I can't help but compare the strategies of incoming senior administrators to those of male lions when they take over a lion pride. In nearly all cases, the first thing that the new dominant male does is kill all the cubs. The explanation given is that he realizes instinctively that he has perhaps three years as the dominant male. If he want to sire his own offspring and raise them to maturity, he can't afford to raise the cubs he finds when he takes over. He needs to kill them, which will bring the lionesses into heat, and then he can sire his own cubs.

Unfortunately, many, if not most, academic administrators behave in a similar manner, ignoring and underfunding the initiatives of their predecessors and redirecting resources into their own programs.[81] Unlike the dominant male lion, however, they are often even indifferent to ensuring that their own initiatives flourish. The reason for this is that their own futures depend more on what is in their resumes than on what actually occurs. Their success depends primarily on the stories they can project. This is one reason why the grants and donations, which end up costing the institution more than they bring in, are still eagerly pursued. A vice president hoping to become a president improves his or her chances of being selected by being able to claim that he or she received a grant for $3 million. The fact that this grant cost more to administer than it brought in doesn't appear anywhere in the resume.

I am personally familiar with a number of variations of such widely acclaimed, but fatally flawed, accomplishments. There was the claimed matching donation of approximately $250,000 from a computer company in connection with the purchase of a large number of computers. The reality was that the computers that were bought not only didn't meet the needs of the institution, but more useful alternative computers could have been purchased for less than the actual money spent. For the vice president who put the deal together, however, the so-called matching deal was preferable because he could claim he had obtained a major contribution.

Then there are the named professorships where the endowments received not only failed to cover the entire cost of the professorship, but didn't begin to cover the additional expenses for support staff, space, and so on. Obviously, such partial endowments are still to be prized if the institution is interested in making the appointments and the appointments are consistent with the objectives of the institutions. If, however, an appointment is unrelated to the basic mission of the institution, the financial drain caused by the appointment is questionable at best.[82] For the administrator procuring such an endowment, however, the only thing that really matters is how it will look on his or her resume. The true long-term costs and implications don't matter because it is highly unlikely that the administrator will be around when the bills need to be paid.

The extent to which the focus of top administrators has switched from the institutions to the administrators' own careers is aptly revealed in a story used by more than one university president. I actually heard a presentation of this story several years ago at a parents' weekend. The college president who made it, I might add, moved on to another institution within a few years.

The setting, as just noted, was a gathering of college freshmen's parents. In an attempt to introduce some humor and also to convey some of the stresses with which he personally lived, the president told the story of the new president who arrives on campus. As he arrives, he meets the previous president who is on his way out. The old president apologizes for not being able to stay around and be of assistance, but he feels it is best that he leave. He then tells the new president that he has left him three envelopes in the back of the center drawer of the president's desk. He explains that he has numbered them one to three and that the new president should use them in that order in dealing with any future crises that might, and probably will, arise.

Sure enough, in his fifth month as president, a crisis arises. The exact nature of the crisis is not described in the story, but faculty, students, and alumni are all protesting. Remembering what his predecessor had told him, the new president goes to his desk and reaches way back in the middle drawer. There he finds three envelopes, with the top one marked "First Crisis." He opens it and reads the following:

> If you are reading this, it means that you are probably in the middle of a crisis and the faculty, students, and alumni are up in arms. Knowing the college as I do, you have probably been there less than six months. I suggest that you tell everyone that you understand and can sympathize with their anger, but having only been there a little while the last thing that they would want you to do is to act impetuously. You, therefore, intend to establish a number of committees to investigate the situation. They can be assured that as soon as these committees report back to you, you will take appropriate action.

The president does as advised and the protest ends.

Approximately a year later the president confronts a second major crisis. Again, with all constituencies screaming for him to act, he goes to the middle drawer of his desk and pulls out the envelope marked "Second Crisis." He opens it and reads the following:

> You are facing your second crisis. Since you have probably been there over a year already, the strategy used last time will not work. What you need to do, therefore, is to tell everyone that not only do you know there is a major problem, but you understand its cause. You hate to say this, but the present crisis is due to gross failures of the previous administration. Unfortunately, the college is like a large ship at sea and cannot be turned around on a dime. You are, however, attempting to correct the mistakes of your predecessor and, hopefully, things will improve soon.

The president follows his predecessor's advice, conveys this information to the college community, and is gratified by their response. The protest ends.

A little more than a year later, the president is confronted with yet another crisis. He confidently retreats to his office and pulls out the envelope marked "Third Crisis." He quickly opens it. The message is very brief. It reads: PREPARE THREE ENVELOPES.

The story is received by the parents and students with laughter and applause.

I appreciate a good story as much as anyone does and this is a good story. It is also, however, a sad commentary on what has happened to higher education or, more specifically, to the leadership of higher education. What tends to be missed when listening to this story is the fact that the crisis of the institution has been supplanted by the crisis of the president. There is no concern here with what might be troubling the institution. There is similarly no concern as to whether the institution confronts a real problem and/or whether there may be real solutions. The only thing that concerns the president is his career. Moreover, our fictional president, and the president who is telling the story, is perfectly happy resolving the first two crises through rhetoric. Unfortunately, educational institutions confront all sorts of real problems that are not resolved through rhetoric.

The more rapid turnover of senior administrators also serves to increase the costs that we earlier noted were associated with external recruitment of such administrators. All the increased costs associated with external searches become magnified when institutions are forced to repeat the process within a few years. Coupled with the increase in numbers of senior administrators, a point we will examine shortly, the rapid turnover of administrators has created a situation where normally one or more searches are going on at any time. This further complicates the whole task of administrating the institution, since the administration is itself in constant flux.

There are other problems associated with this process. One of the most troubling is that it is becoming more and more difficult to obtain reliable information on external candidates. Whatever the drawbacks to internal candidates, one of their advantages is that they are known commodities. People might argue over their strengths and weaknesses, but there are seldom unknown skeletons hidden in closets. Maybe a small bone here and there, but nothing major. This is why people often prefer "the devil they know to the devil they don't know." In academia, however, preferences, at least of those empowered to hire, appear to have gone the other way. The reason may be that whatever skeletons external candidates may have hidden in closets are less likely to be discovered. They are unlikely to be discovered because academic administrators appear to have been successful in legitimating a policy of thwarting inquiry.

One of the key factors in most successful search procedures is gathering as much information as possible about the various candidates. In addition to soliciting letters from references recommended by the candidates, a good search committee obtains information from others familiar with the candidate. This normally includes a number of people who have previously worked with the candidate. It may also entail site visits to the candidate's present or past institutions. Not surprisingly, most candidates have historically attempted to control this process as much as possible in order to direct search committees toward favorable references and hinder their contact with critics. The rapid turnover of senior administrators, however, seems somehow to have institutionalized this preference into present practice. Candidates have been allowed to determine whom search committees can and cannot contact. The argument presented normally is that they would prefer that their present institution not know that they are a candidate for another job and, consequently, they would prefer if the search committee speak only to those whom the candidate indicates. Many candidates go so far as to request that the whole process be kept secret.

In light of the rapid turnover noted earlier, it is not surprising that many, if not most, institutions become irritated when a newly hired administrator becomes a candidate for another position almost before he or she has arrived. On the other hand, those who represent the institution are themselves likely to be in much the same situation. As a result, they tend to respond favorably to the request to maintain confidentiality. What this results in, of course, is a situation in which the candidate has nearly complete control in orchestrating his or her own candidacy. This situation also serves to enhance the inflated, often misleading, list of accomplishments contained in the candidate's résumé. In short, it is a situation tailor-made for self-promotion and duplicity.

The situation has become so extreme that it is more and more common for institutions to require newly hired administrators to commit themselves to remaining for a specific number of years. Unfortunately, like politicians who, having promised to serve out their terms if elected, seek another position in the middle of their term, it is not uncommon for top administrators to renege on such commitments. What is even more troubling is that no one seems to care. In the mid-'90s the trustees of one of the most prestigious New England colleges in the country hired away the newly appointed president of another New England college, even though it was widely known that he had given his word to remain for five years. As this book goes to print, a similar event has occurred with the president of Brown being hired away by Vanderbilt in his second year. Whatever the justification for such behavior, it has a very bad effect on the moral tone of higher education institutions. Moreover, it reflects negatively on those hiring the president—the board of trustees—as much as it does on the president himself.

Even the most cooperative search committee, or senior person or group empowered to make the actual hiring decision, will require more than a candidate's résumé and references selected by the candidate. They will want some independent evaluation. This, however, often turns out to be of questionable value for the institution, if not for those making the appointment. The reason for this is quite simple. To whom are those making the appointments likely to turn? Their equivalents in the other institution, which means the present or past superiors of the candidate.

This fact has not been lost on those seeking higher administrative positions. Ambitious mid-level administrators realize that it is their superiors who can help or hurt them in moving on and up. Whereas truly successful academic administrators are administrators who can motivate and work with faculty and students, promotional success depends more on getting along with senior administrators to whom one reports. While there is no rule that says that an administrator cannot get along well both with those above and those below, the reality is that administrators who fight for those they represent are seldom the favorites of those above. Similarly, the favorites of those above tend to be more concerned with the needs of those above than of the institution itself.

The increased costs and more self-serving character of senior administrators produced by external recruitment, as well as the greater turnover of administrators, would be worrisome by themselves. But, as noted at the beginning of this chapter, more has happened. There has been a dramatic increase in the size of most academic administrations and most of them have also been given greater powers. The two, not surprisingly, are related. What has been the effect of each of these developments?

One of the most significant effects of academic administrative growth has been a correlative increase in costs. Unfortunately, while no one denies that such growth has occurred, it is often difficult to price this growth accurately. One of the main reasons is that academic administration takes various forms that enable the costs to be allocated in different ways. While the great bulk of administrative costs are normally designated institutional support costs, for example, significant administrative costs, such as chairs' salaries and faculty released time for administrative duties, are normally contained under the heading of instructional and research costs. Other administrative costs are allocated to other categories. What is clear, however, is that whereas most higher education institutions functioned with overall administrative costs of 5 percent and less twenty years ago, few function today at less than 10 percent.[83] In part, this has been due to an ever-increasing number of assistant and associate deans, provosts, and vice presidents. It is also due to a dramatic increase in the salaries paid to these individuals in comparison to salaries paid to faculty and lower-level staff personnel.

Twenty years ago, the common practice was to pay academic administrators at their faculty rates, with an added stipend to compensate them for the extra hours and summers that the administrative job entailed. This stipend tended to vary from a few thousand dollars up to 20 percent of their salary. Today, few administrators are paid less than a third more than their academic salaries and many receive more than double what they would earn as a faculty member. The increase for nonacademic administrators has often been even greater. Whereas a few decades ago, the financial business of the college was handled by a bookkeeper and support staff, earning bookkeepers' salaries, the vice president for finance at many institutions earns significantly more than the average full professor's salary. In fact, except for those universities with medical schools and highly paid medical professors, financial vice presidents normally earn more than anyone except the president.[84]

These enlarged administrations have additional costs in the form of various perks. The most costly perks tend to be additional support staff. Where in the past it was common for deans of faculty to work with a single secretary, today they often have a large secretarial staff as well as numerous assistant and associate deans. There are also costs for more elaborate offices, including more expensive office equipment. Many senior administrators are entitled to automobiles and even housing allowances. In addition, increased travel and entertainment budgets are necessary for academic administrators to attend national and international meetings and host visiting guests from foundations and other institutions.

So what do we get for this enlarged, more expensive administration? Primarily, more red tape and other hindrances. Some examples might help to illustrate this process.

Since the late '60s, most institutions of higher education have sought to increase the diversity of their faculty. Clearly, some have tried harder than others, yet few have tried as hard as they have proclaimed. In nearly all cases, however, most institutions established procedures intended to support the hiring of a more diverse faculty. These procedures usually included ensuring that advertisements for all positions had nondiscriminatory disclaimers, that such advertisements were broadly circulated, and that candidate lists were reviewed by an affirmative-action officer.

As a public institution servicing a highly diverse student body, Queens College has had a rigorous and exacting hiring protocol in place for many years. Moreover, at every step of the process a number of different individuals are responsible to ensure that this protocol is honored. These individuals include the department chair, members of the departmental search committee, the college affirmative-action officer, the divisional academic dean, the provost, the human relations officer, and the president.

One would think that this was sufficient overkill for any bureaucratic process. In recent years, however, with the growth of the central City University of New York administration, the central office entered the process and elected to duplicate the various steps taken at the college. One could argue that while such duplication might be unnecessarily expensive and time-consuming, it might also serve as extra insurance. In reality, because the central administrators making the decisions have little to no idea of what the recruitment process of diverse candidates actually involves, their input, more often than not, has been counterproductive.

I can relate one specific example of such a situation. In order to ensure a nondiscriminatory search, it is normal to require that a pool of all candidates be formally constituted and that this pool be certified by the affirmative-action officer before a final group of candidates can be selected for interviews. The objective is to ensure that the candidate pool approximates the distribution of possible candidates.[85] This practice has been in effect for some time. Unfortunately, it suffers from one major drawback. Attractive diversity candidates are usually snapped up quite quickly, often by institutions that are not as burdened by bureaucratic procedures. As a result, serious search committees are usually anxious to have their pool of candidates certified as soon as possible,[86] especially if they have a number of good diversity candidates. A potential problem with this strategy, however, is that once the pool has been certified, no new candidates can be added. Unfortunately, it often happens that once a pool has been certified, other strong candidates appear, including strong diversity candidates.

The rule that late candidates cannot be added to the pool once the pool has been certified is in keeping with the central goal of ensuring a level playing field for all. Without such a rule, it would be possible to limit the number of potential candidates by closing the pool early and then adding a favored candidate later. Historically, such a favorite candidate would likely not have been a diversity candidate, but rather a candidate already known to the committee through existing networks. Even if the late candidate is a diversity candidate, the probabilities are high that other diversity candidates would be excluded.

There is, however, a sound and fair alternative procedure that can deal with situations where an extremely attractive diversity candidate appears after the pool has been certified. The entire pool can be recertified. Admittedly, this entails considerable additional work since it requires going through the entire review process a second, and perhaps a third, time. For a faculty attempting to hire the strongest candidate, the effort has historically been seen as worthwhile. It was quite normal, in fact, for search committees to request that a pool be reconstituted because a number of strong, late candidates materialized. Unfortunately, this not only creates additional work for the administrators who must recertify the new pool, but it also can appear somewhat sloppy and/or inefficient from a purely administrative perspective.

I surmise that it was for such reasons, but I really don't know, that a few years ago the central administration refused to allow the recertification of candidate pools. When it was explained to them in a particular case that this would exclude a highly desirable diversity candidate from being considered, they suggested and approved that a waiver for this particular candidate be given. While the department was pleased to be able to interview the candidate, it was clear to everyone that a rule intended to increase diversity had been interpreted in a way that had the opposite effect. The only way the original objective was satisfied was in breaking the rule. Here we have a clear example of how an added layer of administrative control, imposed primarily as a means for justifying the existence of the administrative layer, not only proved frustrating but served to hinder the very policies it was established to support.

The example just given is not unique. Much of what these enlarged administrative structures do to justify their own existence is require more documentation of the day-to-day activities of the faculty. The key words here tend to be *assessment* and *accountability*. Minimally, this requires faculty to invest more and more time in generating more and more paperwork, taking away time for more important activities. In most cases, this paperwork ends up sitting unread on someone's desk. In those rare cases when significant actions are actually based on such paperwork, however, real damage can be done. Resources can be reallocated and practices modified to meet standards that are actually counterproductive to the overall educational goals.

Few things, for example, have served to lower academic standards more in recent years than heightened administrative pressure to maintain enrollment and graduation rates. Such pressures, coupled with the practice of relying more heavily on student evaluations in judging teaching, make it more difficult for teachers, especially junior faculty, to put high demands on students. It should be stressed that the problem is not the stated objectives of enhancing enrollment, graduation rates, or student satisfaction. The problem lies in the form that such assessment initiatives normally take when generated by a distant administration. More often than not, the assessment instrument created fails to measure what it is intended to measure, or worse, it serves to impede the desired objectives.

While the demand for more assessment and accountability seldom serves the stated objectives, it has served to strengthen overall administrative power by giving administrators another means for interceding in the daily operations of the faculty. Without the ability to demand a continuing stream of reports, few academic administrations, even if they were to double in size, have any hope of imposing control over their institutions. The reason for this is that such administrations are not essential to academic institutions, which have functioned for decades without an extensive supervisory infrastructure. Most academic institutions have rather been managed through a unique collaborative, voluntary governance system that, whatever its limitations, has been remarkably immune to control from above. The demand from above for more reports doesn't in and of itself endow top management with more control over this process, but by providing top management with an added harassment instrument, this clearly enhances its power over the faculty.

Although administrative growth has by and large occurred at the expense of the faculty, it is only fair to note that in many, if not most, institutions the faculty played a role in this growth. Faculty members did not intend to bring about this result, but administrative growth occurred because faculty tried to insulate itself from the various assaults upon higher education described earlier. When confronted with charges of economic inefficiencies, curriculum irrelevancy, and archaic management principles and practices, many educational institutions and their faculties attempted to deflect the criticisms with various types of quick fixes rather than deal with them directly. This generally meant establishing a committee here and adding a course or program there, as well as engaging a few people here and there to manage things more efficiently.

What few faculty members or administrators realized at the time was that they were laying the foundation for the emergence of a new managerial class. Whereas previously the practice of selecting higher administrators from the faculty leadership provided a sufficient number of qualified people, it became more and more necessary to augment the administration ranks from other sources. Deans of faculty became provosts supported by growing legions of associate and assistant provosts. Heads of nonacademic departments became vice presidents with ever growing staffs of human relations and legal experts. More important, this new managerial class rapidly evolved its own interests and agenda, which were and are often unrelated to those of faculty and students. In fact, given that many of this new managerial class's members had not succeeded as academics to the extent that they had intended, it is not surprising that significant chunks of their agenda are not faculty-friendly.[87]

While the increased tension between faculty and administration is widely recognized, few grasp the extent to which the agenda of the new managerial class may often become student-unfriendly. Given that the new managerial class's interest in institutional growth generally translates into the acceptance of increased numbers of students, many observers have assumed otherwise. Such conclusions have also been reinforced by the "student-centered" rhetoric embodied in the 1965 education act that most new administrators articulate. What is often overlooked is the extent to which increased access is linked to different sorts of education, including more vocational and remedial education, and a per-student reduction in educational support. Put slightly differently, access and growth have been financed primarily by lowering per-unit costs by offering less expensive educational products.

Initially, this growth strategy seemed to favor everyone. For the higher education institutions, the increase in numbers increased revenues. It's true that the increased revenues seldom enabled the institution to maintain the overall per-student support that previously existed, but such revenues normally covered increased marginal costs. The strategy also promised to serve various external constituencies better by providing a more well-trained workforce. At the same time, many students previously denied access to higher education would be granted access. The fact that total budgets were increased was normally obfuscated by the fact that real cost per student often declined.

Broadening the educational products offered does complicate things, however. Not only do budgets become more complex, but relations with external constituencies become both more intricate and more important. Many institutions of higher learning, especially public institutions, are no longer left with the simple responsibility of selecting students who can perform adequately once accepted, but they must now establish transitional programs for students who are not yet ready to perform adequately. Educational programs, meanwhile, need to be reviewed regularly in terms of their suitability to workforce demands. Both of these processes, in turn, often entail external funding sources. One of their big attractions is that they are capable of generating such funding. These external funding sources, however, normally entail guidelines of various types bearing on everything from accounting procedures to ethnic and gender demographics. Taken together, they serve to further strengthen the institutional positions of the new class of higher education administrators since they tend to be more willing, if not better able, to deal with such issues.

While the new managerial class has benefited from some of its special skills, its ability to reproduce itself has probably been its major accomplishment. As noted earlier, most higher educational administrators were historically drawn from the very same faculties that they later administered. Although some were selected primarily for their proven administrative skills, others were chosen for the leadership position they had established within the faculty. While a good number also had national and international academic status, this was clearly not always the case. Yet local respect, whatever its basis, was normally a prerequisite.

Today, however, administrative skills and regulative knowledge are the primary requirements. Such skills and knowledge demand greater familiarity with such national issues as diversity, curriculum development, marketing, fundraising, and various entitlement programs. This, in turn, nearly always requires some involvement with national higher education organizations such as the American Council on Education (ACE), the Association of American Colleges and Universities (AAC&U), the American Association of Higher Education (AAHE), the American Council of Academic Deans (ACAD), Council for Advancement and Support of Education (CASE), and the Council of Colleges of Arts and Sciences (CCAS), which focus on such issues.[88] Unfortunately, greater familiarity with an issue can mean little more than greater ability to use the current jargon associated with the issue. It doesn't necessarily mean that the individual understands the issue or is better equipped to manage the issue. It does mean, however, that he or she will appear more knowledgeable during a job interview.

In addition to playing a central role in defining the dominant issues of higher education, these organizations often serve as informal brokers in the recruitment and placement of academic administrators. In part, this is because they tend to be well-connected with most academic headhunters. It is also due to the fact that most of these organizations are involved in one way or another with a wide range of new programs and initiatives, including various diversity initiatives, new management paradigms, and new pedagogical models. They are consequently often in a good position to identify candidates for administrative positions, including diversity and women candidates interested in administrative careers.

These candidates tend to be not only more diverse but also more sensitive to external demands and less committed to traditional academic procedures. Many had administrative experience, though this experience was more likely to be that of a director of a program than the chair of a traditional academic department. With a corresponding dearth of jobs in most traditional academic job markets, there were also sufficient numbers who were both mobile and ready to take on more administrative responsibilities. In a relatively short period of time, many academic administrative functions that had historically been handled on a rotating basis by willing, internally and informally recommended faculty for a course release or a modest stipend were transformed into associate and assistant deanships and staffed through a formal search process that more often than not favored external candidates.

Given the tendency of most faculties to shun administrative responsibilities, these developments occurred by and large with faculty acceptance if not active support. Most faculty members were more than content to let others take care of administrative details, which allowed them to concentrate on their research and teaching. Faculties have historically been accustomed to having their deans and presidents run their colleges and universities with little faculty interference. Academic administrators, for their part, have historically been quite autocratic in the way they have managed their institutions. It was assumed, however, that deans and presidents would administer their institutions in a manner consistent with the interests and beliefs of the faculty. Practically all deans and even most presidents were assumed to embrace the academic worldview. As indicated earlier, many, if not all, of the new administrative class no longer share this worldview.

It should be noted that the administrative changes described herein have also had their positive effects. More attention has been paid to management and financial issues and various innovations have been instituted. There is also significantly more diversity to be found in most administrations. The curriculum has likewise been broadened to include a wider range of perspectives and issues. Most academic institutions have grown more responsive to community needs and more aware of the employment situation confronting their graduates. These are important improvements.

The main drawback to all of these developments is that, like the new managerial class itself, these initiatives remain tangential. They remain tangential because the new administrative class tends to denigrate and ignore the traditional governance structure that made American higher education work. Faculty members are often put in the role of employees, and students are often put in that of consumers. Both groups are commonly seen as adversaries, or at least as others to be managed, rather than as constituencies to be engaged. This results not only in less productive and rewarding programs and policies, but in more expensive programs and policies—just the opposite of what was initially intended. This is why I would judge such administrative growth, as I judged the various cost-cutting and revenue enhancement initiatives in the previous chapter, to be a "faulty cure."

As the various attempts to transform the economics of higher education favored transforming the management and administrative policies and practices of higher education, so these administrative changes have favored transforming higher education's traditional governance and reward structure. It is to these proposed cures that we now turn.

7

∾

Curtailing Traditional Faculty Governance and Reward Systems

The cures described in the previous two chapters—cutting costs, raising revenues, and altering management policies and practices—are meant to achieve specific objectives. The initiatives to be examined in this chapter are somewhat different. Their goal is not to effect a particular desired end or set of ends, but rather to circumvent what are perceived to be hindrances in achieving these ends. What they share in common is the assumption that the major hindrance to aggressive change in higher education is the governance power traditionally held by the faculty. While these initiatives often encompass some of the concrete goals discussed earlier, such as the elimination of tenure and sabbatical leaves, their principal objective is to reduce faculty power over all aspects of institutional life. In so doing, they further seek to make faculty members more accountable for their activities, both in and out of the classroom.

Earlier, it was argued that although tenure has been attacked as an expensive academic practice, it is in reality a very efficient unfunded fringe benefit. As such, eliminating tenure would not only fail to generate savings, it would likely increase costs. This is known and understood by most who defend tenure. Though they seldom admit so publicly, it is also known by most administrative critics of tenure. So why should they attack it? The reason is quite simple. Tenure is not an economic issue. It is a political issue. It isn't about money; it is about power. Tenure gives a faculty member a degree of independence that most employees do not have. This independence can be used effectively to hinder administrative action.

Does this mean that if tenure were eliminated, significant numbers of faculty would lose their jobs? Highly unlikely. As just noted, tenure is an economically efficient practice. The elimination of tenure would, however, afford for greater administrative supervision and control of the faculty. Without tenure, the administration would be in a position to institute more stringent and regular review procedures for all faculty members. While such reviews would seldom lead to termination of employment and though most administrations can institute whatever faculty review processes they would like now, reviews formally tied to reappointments would significantly alter the political balance between the faculty and administration.[89]

Much the same thing can be said for curtailing sabbatical leaves. While critics complain about the cost of such leaves, as noted earlier they generally cost nothing. Many institutions actually save money. As with tenure, however, there are political issues. By converting sabbatical *leaves* into sabbatical *fellowships,* a historic faculty *right* is transformed into an earned faculty award. Faculty are no longer entitled to sabbatical leaves. They must present a reasonable case to justify a leave. Again, as with tenure, it is unlikely that substantially fewer sabbatical leaves would be awarded under such a new system, if for no other reason than that they are economically advantageous to the institution. On the other hand, the process of granting them as awards rather than as rights increases the supervisory powers of the administration, since the administration can use the threat of denial to obtain other objectives.

The desire to increase the supervisory authority of the administration over the faculty is embedded in another practice that many proponents of institutional change champion, namely, the greater use of merit pay. This is a practice that we have not yet discussed because even its most ardent supporters rarely propose merit pay as a cost-saving device. In contrast, it is advanced almost exclusively in terms of the greater supervisory powers that it affords the administration. Not only does it provide a means to financially reward faculty members who cooperate with the administration and punish those who resist, but it also favors establishing a whole evaluation system to support and justify salary decisions. If faculty members are to be paid based upon their performance, then performance must be evaluated, which requires a system of close observation and review. If the existing merit pay system can be used as a model, salary increases are unlikely to change in any dramatic way. Pay increases will continue to be distributed equally across the faculty and little weight will be given to the review process. Nevertheless, the very existence of such a system enhances the power that the administration has over its faculty.

While faculty members may not like being forced to concede greater power to the administration, one could argue that such a transfer of power is in the overall interest of the institution. Many, if not all, administrators make such claims. There are sound reasons to believe, however, that such a reallocation of power is highly counterproductive in the long run. It is counterproductive insofar as most institutions of higher education are *voluntary* organizations dependent upon a governance structure supported and maintained by volunteer labor.[90] Actions that alienate faculty and hence thwart volunteer faculty initiatives are shortsighted at best.

This is not to deny that the faculty is paid. Faculty members are paid contractually, however, primarily to teach and to carry on their research. The fact that they are also expected to manage themselves, oversee large aspects of the institution, and be responsible for innumerable other processes and activities is contractually highly ambiguous. Without these extra activities, which are dependent upon the faculty's *voluntary* contributions of time and effort, most higher education institutions could not function.

In forcing the faculty into the role of employees and subordinates, the administration and its allies, in effect, enable faculty members to abandon some of their historic responsibilities. Initially, an administration may judge such losses as more than offset by the greater administrative freedom derived from "putting the faculty in its place." The administration happily takes on the new responsibilities, hires additional support staff to do the day-to-day work, and rejoices in being free from the need to collaborate with the faculty. Unfortunately, not only does this strategy entail significantly increased costs, as more and more administrators and support staff are added to the payroll to do the job that the faculty once did freely, but the new administrators and support staff generally prove to be inadequate for the task. A few concrete examples may help to illustrate the dynamics of such situations.

Student advisement has historically been primarily a faculty obligation. In their capacity as advisers, the faculty was responsible for advising students on a wide range of issues, including what courses they should take, which extracurricular activities might be helpful, employment opportunities, and, to a varying extent, life in general. While nearly all faculty members had such advisement responsibilities, some took them more seriously than others. Moreover, some fulfilled these responsibilities better than others did. Even those who tended to shirk their advisement duties, however, generally accepted the judgment that student advisement constituted part of their overall professorial responsibilities. Such shirkers also normally were subject to peer criticism and pressure. At the same time, the slack created by such shirkers was normally "covered" by their more responsible colleagues.

For the most part, college and university administrators historically responded to this situation with a combination of minor rewards for the exceptionally responsible and criticism for the most egregious shirkers. The situation has changed substantially in recent years, due in large part to administrative growth. The broadly recognized limitations of the faculty system, coupled with the comfort that many administrators have with advisement, has given rise to a transfer of responsibility with which both the administration and the faculty have concurred.

For the administrators this has made sense, insofar as advisement is an activity for which administrators can usually claim equal, if not superior, qualifications than faculty. They often have greater student activity experience than most faculty,[91] more knowledge of the various offerings of the college or university as a whole, and more interest and knowledge of external employment opportunities. Given the career ambitions of most members of the new administrative class, there is the added attraction of instituting a new program that can be highlighted on one's résumé, to say nothing of the more traditional bureaucratic activity of *empire building*. If all of this was not enough, an administration that elects to relieve the faculty of a large part of its advisement responsibilities can claim that it is also assisting the faculty. As far as most faculty are concerned, transferring advisement to the administration simply relieves them of another burden.

So what is the problem? First and foremost, it doesn't work as intended. Even when additional administrators are hired, both the quality and quantity of advisement tends to decline. Moreover, what becomes clear very quickly is that even when a sizable number of people are hired exclusively to act as student advisers, advisement per se still requires the backing of the faculty for much of the day-to-day advisement required. In fact, more often than not, what happens is that the newly hired advisers become the new managers of the old system. While they may have a better overview of what courses the college offers, for example, they don't have sufficiently expert knowledge of the offerings within a given department to know which of two or three different courses would be most appropriate for a given student. They are forced, therefore, to send the student back to the department for additional faculty advisement.

A two-step, or even three-step, advisement process, in and of itself, wouldn't seem to be such a bad idea. Unfortunately, it ignores the fact that students are not only bad at seeking out advice, they also don't like following it. Commonly, those students most in need of advice are least able and willing to obtain it. It is often difficult enough to get them to go to a single advisement session, let alone to meet with a number of different people. Second, the faculty is often not so willing to function in this back-up role. As difficult as it can be to get some faculty members to accept their advisement responsibilities under the traditional system, it is even more difficult when they can argue that advisement is not their responsibility but rather the responsibility of the administration. As a result, the few faculty members who traditionally would have taken on the great bulk of advisement responsibilities often find themselves with an even greater proportion of this responsibility when an administrative advisement office exists. Moreover, even these faculty members tend to resent that significant sums of money are being spent to support activities that they do for free.

A second related area, where a somewhat similar scenario is commonly played out, is tutoring and mentoring. While faculty members are expected to work individually with students wherever appropriate, most faculty members look upon such activities as "extras." It is the volunteer syndrome again.

This is understandable, since they practically never receive additional remuneration for such activities and most of their fellow faculty members manage to avoid taking on such extra work. As a consequence, and similarly to what happens with advisement, the responsibility and burden of providing tutorial and mentoring supervision falls unequally on the shoulders of a few.

While most administrations are supportive of faculty mentoring and tutorial activities, they are often hesitant to provide resources to compensate faculty members who take on such added responsibilities, let alone invest additional resources to increase such activities. This is understandable from an administrative perspective because both mentoring and tutorials, despite strong evidence of their educational value, are very expensive.[92] It also doesn't make sense to invest in such programs as part of a co-optation, empire-building effort, since these activities are dependent on academic expertise. As a consequence, most administrations restrict themselves to providing moral and verbal support for such activities. Unfortunately, such support, when coupled with the overall growth and muscle flexing of the administration, more often than not proves to be counterproductive. The reason for this is quite simple. Mentoring and tutoring do entail additional, voluntary efforts on the part of the faculty. Such efforts are much less likely to be forthcoming when the administration is seen as attempting to dominate the faculty.

Such negative, sometimes uncooperative, faculty behavior is the heavy cost that many institutions of higher education pay as a result of the new administrative class's attempt at domination. It affects not only supplemental activities such as advising, mentoring, and tutoring, but such day-to-day activities as service on committees, departmental administrative activities, and overall collaborative efforts. Something as central as scheduling, for example, can be made more difficult.

Scheduling is one of those administrative activities that academic departments have discharged efficiently on a voluntary, self-managed basis for decades. Admittedly, in most cases the process is quite simple since the schedule remains pretty much the same from semester to semester and from year to year. There are, however, always some conflicts concerning which courses will be offered in a given semester, at what time, and taught by whom, which result in the request of a certain faculty member not being fully met. In most cases these situations are resolved through a process of informal barter, in which an attempt is made to maintain overall equity over the long run. If faculty member X, for example, is given an unattractive schedule in a given semester, he or she will be favored with a more attractive schedule the next semester. The whole process is supported by the faculty's assumption that the chair is doing his or her best to meet the needs of the faculty as well as the requests of students and administration.

This assumption and resulting cooperation can, and often does, disappear if the faculty believes that the administration is attempting to meddle in what it believes are departmental decisions. Particularly irritating to faculty, but tempting to administrators, are attempts to use faculty schedules to ensure that faculty will be on campus for more hours and days per week. Many in the new administrative class will argue that it is their responsibility to "extend" the time faculty members are on campus. Most faculty see this not only as illegitimate, but as vindictive, reflecting administrators' frustration and resentment over the fact that they—administrators—are expected to be on campus the entire workweek.

Whatever the true grounds for such actions, faculty members often respond to attempts to increase their time on campus by withdrawing the cooperation previously extended. They can do this in all sorts of ways, including simply refusing to accept certain classes assigned to them, to missing more classes, to driving students out of their classes with heavier than normal work assignments. Whatever the means of defiance, the result is that unilateral administrative attempts to generate more attractive and balanced schedules more often than not produce just the opposite result. In defense of the faculty, it should be noted that their defiance is often much more than a refusal to conform to administrative edicts. Usually, there are sound reasons for maintaining the schedule that is in place, which has often evolved through trial and error over many years.

As discomfiting as faculty defiance can be, its negative institutional consequences are trivial in comparison to other types of faculty responses. A defiant faculty remains an institutionally committed faculty. Much more disturbing is a faculty that simply retreats. Many an administration in conflict with its faculty might long for such a withdrawn faculty, but in the long run a combative faculty is much less destructive than a disengaged faculty. The reason for this is the inherently voluntary character of institutions of higher education noted earlier. No academic administration, not even the comparatively bloated administrations that have emerged on campuses during the last decade, is capable of managing its institutions on its own. An academic administration doesn't have the personnel, the expertise, the knowledge, or any of a dozen other prerequisites to go it alone. When the faculty withdraws, the institution loses not only its sight, its hearing, its touch, its smell, its taste, but also most of its common sense. In short, a bullying administration will not have the range of honest feedback required to manage efficiently.

There are other costs entailed in driving the faculty to the sidelines. Administrators may like to believe that they represent their institutions and in some arenas they do. The main reputation of any institution of higher education, however, isn't based on the quality and standing of its administrators, but on the eminence and prestige of its faculty. Moreover, the public tends to take what administrators say about their own institution, especially when it is positive, with the proverbial grain of salt. In contrast, they tend to take much more seriously the evaluations of the faculties. A disgruntled, annoyed, withdrawn faculty can hurt the image of an educational institution more quickly and more seriously than any other group. Moreover, their negativism can, and generally will, also serve to drive away attractive new faculty members, leading to the further weakening of the institution.

What makes these negative repercussions of administrators' attempts to dominate faculty even more destructive is the fact that they tend to feed and encourage the behavior that caused them in the first place. Few administrators respond to faculty resistance and withdrawal by rethinking their basic strategy. Quite the contrary. Most use these responses as proof that the initial strategy was correct but needs to be intensified. What follows often is nothing less than a full-fledged faculty-bashing campaign, followed not unexpectedly by greater faculty resistance and so on. This is generally accompanied by a loss of reputation, followed by a loss of funds. Not a very attractive scenario, but a more common one than is commonly acknowledged.

The conflict between administrators and faculty has other negative ramifications. One of the more costly, but subtler and less obvious, consequences has been a general decline in academic collegiality. Despite the fact that academics often have the reputation, especially among administrators, of being self-centered, the traditional structure of colleges and universities has fostered a more collaborative milieu than that of most other settings. The very word *collegiate* reflects this fact. This is not to deny that academics, as a group, are highly self-absorbed in their own interests and work. The comparatively lonely existence of a scholar, who is forced to spend most of his or her working hours alone, listening to a highly personal muse, requires a high degree of self-discipline and self-motivation. Coupled with this self-centered work orientation, however, is a high degree of social solidarity that serves to reinforce a common "faculty" worldview as well as many "faculty" interests. It is as if the highly individualized nature of faculty members' work requires a more encompassing social ethic.

The traditional tension between the faculty and the administration has frequently served to reinforce this collegiality. The common administrative adversary often serves to draw an otherwise disparate faculty together. When resources become very scarce and conflicts intensify, there is a tendency for such alliances to break down. This will most likely happen when conditions allow some in the group to protect themselves and even prosper if they elect to abandon their group, if not actually collaborate with the opposition. These are exactly the conditions that a number of administrators have created and are creating intentionally and accidentally on our college and university campuses, as they micromanage scarce resources. Such micromanagement initiatives include not only a greater use of merit pay, but differential teaching loads, research support, better offices, more modern computers, and so forth. The broad objective of nearly all such efforts is to acquire the right to reward faculty more individually.

The claimed objective of a more individualized reward system is to make the faculty more responsive and productive. Unfortunately, for many of the reasons already noted the system does not permit this to happen. Whatever gains are produced as a result of greater individual efforts stimulated by this strategy are more than offset by losses due to the decline in collaboration. What is perhaps even more troubling, however, is the fact that such a strategy can and often does have additional negative side effects. Not only does it often generate a high degree of counterproductive faculty self-promotion and communal deterioration, it can also serve to redirect faculty and institutional efforts into unproductive, questionable directions.

In light of the attention given to economic factors by the new administrative class, it should come as no surprise to learn that from the administrative perspective, faculty efforts that generate resources are highly prized. Many faculty members are admittedly also interested in obtaining financial resources. From a traditional faculty perspective, however, financial resources are less prized than major academic products. The grant is great, but the real payoff is the research monograph produced because of the grant. Genuine prestige is still tied to scholarly success. For many in the new administrative class, it is the money that counts and the money that they are willing to reward. This emphasis on monetary goals can create the change of direction noted earlier.

Clearly, other factors are at work in this change of direction. The most important of these is the source of potential resources. Where is the money to come from? A large percentage of potential funds resides with the federal government and its various agencies, as it has since the end of World War II. Other large chunks reside with the major foundations supporting humanistic, scientific, social, and educational research programs. More recently, significant sums of money, often in the form of fairly specific contractual arrangements, have become available from the corporate sector. What is true of all of these resources is that they have tended to become more practical and programmatic in recent years. There are still funds to support basic research, but much less in comparison to even twenty years ago.

Where does this leave the ambitious academic? In a position quite similar to that of the ambitious administrator. Rather than seeking support for a particular scholarly project, faculty members find that the situation often favors their reframing a project to make it eligible for existing funds. The hope, of course, is that there will be sufficient funds to support the original scholarly project as well as the more applied project. As with the grants sought by the administrators discussed in the previous two chapters, it often turns out that the institution ends up losing resources in the end, rather than benefiting. In addition, the very mission of the institution is often redefined, if not compromised. For the faculty member, however, obtaining such grants and contracts can serve not only to enhance his or her résumé, but also to obtain additional rewards from the administration.

Curtailed faculty independence and governance rights, coupled with the resulting loss of faculty loyalty, followed commonly by administrative faculty-bashing and often faculty resistance, have generated yet other institutional schisms, including those associated with the formation and functioning of academic unions.

Thirty years ago few faculties were unionized. Most faculty members belonged to the American Association of University Professors, the AAUP, which served primarily as a professional association. As such, it was concerned with issues of academic freedom and proper academic protocol bearing on academic tenure, hiring and promotion policies, and so forth. The AAUP did not get involved in salary negotiations or, for that matter, most financial or administrative issues. These were left to the individual institutions and faculty representatives to negotiate, insofar as any negotiations occurred at all. In most cases, these issues were simply decided by the administration. The only "protection" faculty members had, or at least felt they had, was the fact that the administrators making the decisions were "one of them."

Since then, a growing number of campuses have elected to form or join a union. During the 1970s the two major umbrella organizations were the National Education Association (NEA) and the American Federation of Teachers (AFT). Both of these organizations, then as well as now, were more heavily engaged in K–12 unions. In the early 1980s the AAUP restructured itself into a professional union, which is now engaged in all the activities that unions are normally engaged in, including salary negotiations and so on. While these organizations often compete with each other in representing different institutions, a number of institutions have maintained joint membership. The CUNY union, the Personnel Staff Congress, for example, belonged to both the AFT and NEA from 1972 through 1975. Since 1981, it has belonged to both the AFT and the AAUP.

From the very beginning of the rise of academic unions, there was an awareness, and even some uneasiness, of potential jurisdictional conflicts between not only the union and the administration, but between the union and the established faculty governance structures. In nearly all cases, these tensions were successfully resolved, with the unions restricting their activities to remuneration, job classification and security, workload, grievance, and due process issues. The traditional faculty governance structures maintained their control over curriculum and pedagogical issues, faculty evaluations, tenure, promotion, and institutional mission. Although unions tended to deal solely with administrations, the existing faculty governance structure often served as an informal buffer between the union and the administration.

The assault by administrations on the faculty and traditional faculty governance rights has changed this situation dramatically. It has generally not
served, as some might have expected, to bring unions and faculty governance groups closer together. Just the opposite. While this might initially
seem surprising, it becomes understandable upon reflection. As just noted,
there has always been some tension between the union and the more traditional governance groups over their mutual rights and responsibilities. The
two groups have also tended to favor different styles, with the unions seeing
themselves in a more confrontational relationship with the administration
and governance leaders seeing themselves in a more collaborative relationship. As a result, each group has responded differently to the administrative
onslaught. Whereas the union has generally cried for greater confrontation,
governance leaders have sought to avoid confrontation. This has created a
situation where each group often ends up accusing the other group of counterproductive behavior.

More than one administration has responded to such splits with jubilation.
In the long run, however, there is nothing to celebrate even from the perspective of administrators. With the loss of a viable governance structure,
unions tend to become more radicalized. Administrations, for their part, tend
to become more confrontational. In the meantime, the mechanisms for generating the types of collaborative decisions required to manage the institution disappear. The institution in most cases continues to function, because,
as noted earlier, colleges and universities are made up primarily of self-
governing and self-generating units, namely, academic classes, departments,
and programs. The collapse of the infrastructure, caused by the previously
described splits and confrontations, however, leaves the institution in a most
precarious situation where any problem, even a fairly minor one, can lead to
a major disruption.

I am sure that some people may read this as nothing more than the proverbial doomsday lament of someone who doesn't like the direction in which
things are going and longs for the good old days of collaboration. Admittedly, there may be elements of such nostalgia in what I have to say. Nevertheless, I would argue that the cause for alarm is real. Moreover, we don't
need to look far to see warning signs of what can happen in such situations.
One needs only to examine foreign higher education systems that lack established faculty governance systems.

There are significant differences among the various systems of higher education to be found around the world. What is relevant to this particular discussion, however, is the extent to which those systems that are most commonly compared favorably to the American system tend to have a highly
developed faculty governance system, whereas those lacking such a governance system are normally ranked as inferior. The fact that the American
higher education system, in contrast to our K through 12 system, is admired

worldwide is commonly attributed to the numbers and involvement of well-trained faculty. It is to the credit of this system that although students who enter generally do so years behind their European counterparts educationally, they emerge four years later as comparative equals. The transformation is so dramatic that the standards of American graduate schools are generally considered to be the highest in the world.

This link between faculty governance and international eminence is further supported by the fact that the most respected foreign higher education institutions such as Oxford and Cambridge and the various Grand Ecoles of France exhibit a similar, if not greater, degree of faculty governance. The faculties of these institutions not only control curriculum, tenure, and promotion, as do American faculties, but admission and many financial decisions. In contrast, the administratively and politically controlled higher education systems of many other countries, such as Italy, survive almost exclusively because of the excellent training that students have previously received in the equivalent of our K to 12 system. In these systems, the faculty tends to be indifferent, if not often hostile, to the students and the administration. This attitude tends to be reciprocated by both students and administrators, both of whom seldom get on that well with each other, either. Strikes and other forms of disturbances are fairly common.

The American symphony scene is also instructive in this context.[93] We seldom make the connection between higher education and symphonies, but there are a number of important organizational similarities. In both cases, the ongoing day-to-day activities of the institution are dependent upon the efforts of a highly trained group of specialists. Without musicians and professors, there would be no orchestras or universities. These specialists are primarily responsible for establishing their own performance programs, selecting their own membership, and coordinating their activities with certain external players such as guest performers. On the other hand, major aspects of administering both institutions are turned over to a group of professional managers. More specifically, these managers are responsible for most fiscal matters, as well as for the formal relationships with external participants, be they students, audiences, or trustees.

Where these two institutions are similar is that both can only function properly when there is collaboration between the musicians/professors and managers/administration. The musicians and professors are responsible for the actual performance, but the administrators are responsible for ensuring that the necessary funds are available to support the performance. This generally means that they are also responsible for soliciting the necessary support, which requires that they have an understanding of what the market desires. They also need to be sensitive to what their performers are able to deliver and, equally important, what they are willing to deliver. If trust breaks down, the performers are likely to seek, usually through union demands and threats, remuneration and other types of support that the administrators cannot generate. On the other hand, if administrators ignore their performers through unilateral management edicts, they are apt to schedule programs that the performers are either unable or unwilling to deliver. In either case, the institution will be unable to fulfill its mission.

Over the years American institutions of higher education have evolved the governance structures capable of dealing with these tensions. Most symphony organizations have not. What is ironic is that at the same time that these symphonic organizations are attempting to create workable governance structures, many academic administrators are in the process of destroying an administrative structure that has worked successfully for generations. Has it been perfect? Clearly not. Most of the criticisms made by administrators have merit. Faculty governance systems do tend to be slow-moving. They do tend to reject change. More important, they have failed to rapidly correct past problems such as curriculum and staffing inequities. This hesitation to move rapidly, however, is due to the system's voluntary, collaborative governance structure rather than to any particular ideological or political bent. Moreover, usually there are reasons to proceed slowly, as was noted earlier regarding the disastrous consequences of many of the market-oriented initiatives pursued by administrators over the objections of the faculty.

This hesitancy to change has also served, whether one likes it or not, to make most of the debate over political correctness irrelevant to what is actually happening on campus. In recent years, political critics, primarily from the right, have complained about what they see as a loss of academic standards and an incursion on the curriculum of ideologically suspect materials. In fact, remarkably little has changed, due to the temperamental conservatism of most faculties. And while most of the complaints have been directed at the faculty, what changes have occurred tend to be the result of administrative efforts. Moreover, while these critics have portrayed these "degrading" changes as due to faculty efforts to use education as a vehicle for political/social change, whatever degrading has occurred was more often than not due to administrative efforts to make higher education more economically relevant.

The classics celebrated by Allan Bloom in *The Closing of the American Mind* aren't being replaced primarily with Third World novels and social science courses on gay lifestyles, but with accounting, computer, and various business and workplace courses. Ironically, the classical liberal arts and science curriculum, with its emphasis on critical thinking, writing skills, and broad-based knowledge, augmented by Third World novels and critical studies of varying sorts, remains the best training for individuals interested in middle- and upper-management positions. In contrast, the preprofessional-oriented education being pushed by so many tracks students into service and lower management positions that often become phased out within a decade. It is seldom the faculty that is behind these developments, however, but rather academic administrators and faculty critics who argue that higher education needs to be made more germane to future employment opportunities.

Here it should be stressed that not all new programmatic initiatives have been academically unsound. Many of the programs introduced, especially many interdisciplinary programs and those dealing with areas previously ignored, enriched the academic curriculum. It should also be noted that there was and remains plenty in the traditional academic curriculum that deserves to be changed. It is highly unlikely, however, that meaningful long-term change will be generated by attempts to make the curriculum more sensitive to future employment needs. It is similarly unlikely that higher education will be improved by making it either more or less "politically correct." Above all, higher education will not benefit from the many and varied attempts to undercut the faculty's role and authority. Whatever else might be true about an institution's faculty, it represents by far the greatest resource of the institution. Collaborative leadership, by encouraging greater commitment and energy from the faculty, can maximize this resource. Faculty-bashing will only serve to minimize it.

I cannot close this chapter without pointing out an ironic twist to the various efforts to undercut the "volunteer" structure of higher education and the associated use of faculty governance, in the name of greater sensitivity to market efficiency. The fact is that the traditional antihierarchical character of American higher education has historically embodied market principles to a greater degree than have most institutions. This market mentality is commonly only recognized insofar as it is revealed in the market of ideas. Yet the broad tendency to allow all participants to have their say and to allow resolutions to emerge through unfettered interaction is essentially how markets function. Admittedly, these same faculty members often appear hostile to such principles when they are applied to the allocation of resources. There is no reason, however, that this need be the case.

Part III

The Promise of Unexploited Market Resources

8

～

Real Issues Confronting
Higher Education

American higher education confronts problems that transcend the false diagnoses and faulty cures described in this book. While these problems come in various shapes and forms, the great majority are due in one way or another to a single phenomenon, namely, the dramatic growth in higher education during the last few decades. More specifically, I would suggest that most of these problems are a result of a thoughtless and unplanned mixing together of very different educational products in response to this growth. This paste-and-mix growth has resulted in a hodgepodge of programs that defy rational categorization, let alone rational management and evaluation. The resulting mish-mash makes it difficult to judge not only the educational value of individual components but their true costs. It is consequently impossible to determine what, if any, economically or educationally more efficient alternate methods might be used to implement particular elements of the total mix.

Some of the roots of this situation have been noted earlier. In searching for additional revenues, many administrators grafted onto their basic educational program various auxiliary programs such as weekend and evening programs. Other programs were added in response to perceived student needs and requests, especially those related to the world of work and remedial courses. Other courses and programs have been added as a way of dealing with demands for a more inclusive curriculum. Technological developments have also served to complicate matters, with additional courses and programs being added to ensure that students are familiar with modern technology. All of this has been accompanied by an infusion of numerically more demographically diverse students with a broader range of academic skills than their predecessors.

While it can be argued that this profusion of programs and students has served to enrich American higher education, like many rich dishes it can cause indigestion. The problem is further complicated by the fact that, to continue with the analogy, too many cooks tend to be in the kitchen, with each cook lobbying for his or her favorite dish and mixture of ingredients. Moreover, there really is no practical way for an outsider, or even an internal arbiter, to get the information needed to evaluate how these diverse components contribute to the total package, let alone what the components are monetarily worth. Such knowledge is generally restricted to the particular experts, who tend to keep what they know to themselves, especially if their information can be used against their interests. As a consequence, it is all but impossible to correct the particular product mix.

The only way to get a handle on the problem is to start at the beginning—to do what, in the context of most organizations, is referred to as zero-base budgeting. This requires selecting, evaluating, and pricing components one by one. In the case of higher education, however, before we can, or rather should, evaluate and cost components, we need to know what we want and what we have. Not surprisingly, one of the first things that we discover is that there is a good deal of disagreement regarding both questions. We already know that a hodgepodge of different programs exists, so let's begin with what we apparently want.

What is the mission of higher education? While numerous answers have been offered, a number of key components seem to be included in nearly all mission statements. Other commonly cited components tend to be particular to only some mission statements. Since our subject is American higher education in general, I think it makes sense initially to be as inclusive, eclectic, and catholic as possible. The list is not numbered since the order of presentation is not intended to rank these items in importance.

Higher education should:

transmit to students accepted knowledge;
pursue and generate knowledge;
preserve and nurture received knowledge;
evaluate proposed knowledge;
expose students to the diversity of knowledge;
train students in critical thinking;
provide students with various cognitive skills;
prepare students for future study;
prepare students for lifelong learning;
prepare students for employment;
provide students with necessary technological skills;
prepare students for citizenship;
stimulate/provide students with a moral and ethical perspective;

expose students to the diversity of the world;
teach students to appreciate their bodies as well as their minds;
prepare students for life;
be accessible to all;
be a knowledge resource for the general society;
be a general cultural resource for the general society;
function as cultural mediator for the general society;
certify and credentialize its students;
provide future civic, economic, and political leaders.

Even this extensive list is not exhaustive, but it does serve to indicate the many and varied objectives built into most mission statements and the variability of what higher education is expected to accomplish. What it does not reflect is the extent to which these various objectives are themselves intertwined and the multiple forms that each can take. More important, it does not prioritize the various objectives. Most important, it doesn't indicate how any of these things is to be accomplished. This brings us to the next question.

How is higher education to do what it is supposed to do? Here again, there are various, often discordant, answers. In an attempt to be inclusive and catholic, we would minimally have to recognize the following pedagogical procedures, support mechanisms, and administrative procedures:

Student readings, including required readings
Student recitations and other oral presentations
Faculty lectures
Student and faculty experimentation
Student and faculty discussions and debates
Student writing
Exams
Training in and access to technology, especially computer technology
Training in and access to various knowledge resources: libraries, Internet, and so forth
Interaction with a mixed and diverse population of students and faculty
Travel
Faculty and student mentoring
Financial aid; jobs, loans, scholarships
Fair admission criteria
Access and available courses for qualified students
Alumni activities
Student, faculty, alumni, and community networks
Research and scholarship
Public forums and lectures
Participation in sports, music, art

There are obviously different degrees of fit between these many and varied procedures and resources and the many and varied objectives noted earlier. Some of the procedures and resources are more directly related to educating students, for example, while others are more related to the production of knowledge. Nearly all of them, however, implicitly if not explicitly, interject a factor not noted in discussing the various missions of higher education—namely, cost. Every item listed requires economic support of some sort, be it the cost of faculty, buildings, books, computers, research equipment, or supplies. Moreover, these costs can and do vary considerably. As a consequence, the overall cost of the education provided will vary considerably, depending upon not only which elements are included, but also on the form of that element included and how these elements are prioritized.

To give a few examples: The faculty instruction costs of an institution that elects to combine lectures and recitations together in a manner that generates a student/faculty ratio of ten students per one faculty member might be five times higher than the faculty instruction costs of an institution that utilizes only large lectures and generates a student/faculty ratio of fifty to one. Similarly, an institution that is primarily interested in transmitting received technical knowledge to its students may be able to utilize a computer-based dissemination system capable of servicing numerous students with little to no faculty support. On the other hand, an institution requiring the critical evaluations of the material by students will require significant faculty participation. There are similar cost differences in supporting different types of student interaction. Simple lounges set aside for minimum student interaction on a commuter campus are considerably less expensive than full-blown residential facilities provided to students attending elite residential colleges. Much the same can be said about the types of support given to exposure to music and arts, participation in athletics, travel opportunities, the generation of original research, and community involvement.

Before cost demands can be properly evaluated, therefore, it is first necessary to decide what educational mix or what range of mixes will be provided. We need to honestly calculate the cost of the various elements, as well as suitable alternatives that constitute the different mixes. In doing this, we also need to recognize that while these various components can be treated individually, various affinities exist that generate natural clusters. This natural affinity factor does not prohibit adding a special element here and there to spice up a given program or cutting a particularly expensive element out of another mix to save resources. An overall rational strategy is needed, however, or we will end up with a final product in which the whole is worth a lot less than the sum of its parts.

This sort of selection process has been implicitly at work on college and university campuses for generations as our various types of higher education institutions have evolved. Unfortunately, with the greater attention given to higher education in recent years, there has been an increase in what might be called selected breeding and attempts at novel grafting. We have already had the opportunity to review some of these efforts and their negative results. Past failures, however, are no excuse for doing nothing. As politically disagreeable as differentiating and pricing the varied programs grouped under the heading of higher education may be, there is no other way out of the quagmire we have created. Once we have done this, we can move on to the next equally demanding issues of determining which mixes make sense, what numbers and proportions of students should be provided access to which types of education, and, finally, how we are to fund the entire package.

As with many difficult questions, the overriding problem we confront isn't an absence of answers, but rather an overabundance of answers. Nearly everyone who has been involved in higher education has his or her own opinion as to what needs to be done. While I am no different than most others in this respect, I am convinced after a lifetime in higher education that no answer or solution, no matter how sound and rational, can or should be imposed on the system by any individual or group. Rather, what I have referred to as the voluntary/market character of higher education requires that any design be openly and thoroughly discussed and debated by all constituencies if such a design is to be implemented. On the other hand, given that even exploratory discussions and deliberations need to begin somewhere, I believe that a number of suggestions can be tentatively presented.

Although the objectives of higher education presented in this chapter are numerous, it is possible to group them in terms of three prime objectives: (1) cultivating properly schooled students; (2) generating knowledge and making such knowledge broadly available; and (3) helping to reproduce civil society. Put slightly differently, the basic products of higher education are students, knowledge, and society itself. Each of these primary outputs, however, can and does take a slightly different form.

In the instance of students, higher education is expected to provide society with students capable of functioning and fitting into the existing society, especially its economic system. It is also expected to produce society's future leaders, people capable of critiquing and changing society. In the case of knowledge, higher education is expected to generate both useful—that is, socially and economically pragmatic—knowledge and basic, pure knowledge. As far as its responsibility in helping to reproduce society, higher education is expected to be both the guardian of received knowledge and customs and also one of the major forces for responsible social change. The more extensive list presented earlier can be fitted to these prime goals as follows.

In order to produce students capable of meeting the job expectations they are likely to confront, higher education needs to provide students with various cognitive skills, teach them the necessary technological skills, and transmit to them accepted knowledge. In addition, if time and resources are adequate, the educational experience should also expose students to the diversity of knowledge, train them in critical thinking, and prepare them for future study and lifelong learning.

The situation and associated responsibilities are somewhat different when it comes to preparing "future leaders." Here, those things commonly seen as the extras in training students for employment become the essentials and the essentials become the extras. More specifically, when it comes to future leaders, higher education needs first and foremost to train students in critical thinking, to transmit to them accepted knowledge, to expose them to the diversity of knowledge, to provide them with various cognitive skills, and to prepare them for future study and lifelong learning. In addition, if time and resources are available, their educational experience should also attempt to aid them for future employment by providing them with necessary technological skills. In both cases, it is also desirable that higher education prepare students for citizenship and provide them, or better help them to provide for themselves, with a moral and ethical perspective. Finally, all of these components should somehow be ascertained and the institution should certify and credentialize its students. It does this primarily by awarding students a degree and graduating them.

Here it might be argued that higher education should provide both types of education to all students. While this might be true in the best of all possible worlds, it doesn't work very well in the world in which we find ourselves. It doesn't work because these two different types of education necessitate different procedures that, in turn, demand different resources. More precisely and more to the point, what might be called critical-thinking education, which has historically been at the core of liberal learning, is a significantly more expensive product than most focused technological/employment training. This becomes self-evident when we look at what is required of the different types of education.

Empowering students to engage in critical and creative thinking requires equipping them with the necessary educational resources. More specifically, they need to be provided with the information, knowledge, and erudition relevant to the issues under examination. This dictates not only exposure to proper required texts but access to appropriate supporting materials. Such access, in turn, requires today not only appropriate library facilities and laboratories and the skills to use these facilities, but also access to the Internet and the skills to use these facilities. Given that at any time, much relevant material exists primarily in oral form, students also require exposure to an informed faculty.

Critical and creative thinking demands more than exposure to information, knowledge, and erudition. It requires an ability to manage, manipulate, compare, contrast, and order ideas. This means that students must be actively engaged in the learning experience. Students must not merely be placed in the role of passive learners. They need continuing opportunities to present their ideas to others in both written and oral form. In many cases, they must also have a chance to experiment with different formulations and ideas. In all of these situations they need to be both challenged and supported. Consequently, these various learning experiences must occur under the supervision and tutelage of a knowledgeable mentor.

While a well-trained mentor can sometimes, in some situations, supervise a fairly large number of students at the same time, this is generally not the case. Good supervision and tutelage generally require close attention. Whereas a faculty person may be able to transmit knowledge to hundreds of students at a given time in a lecture, the supervision and tutelage entailed in fostering critical and creative thinking are limited to comparatively few students at any given time. Ideally, a faculty person functioning in this role is expected to supervise no more than a dozen students at once. When the numbers grow much beyond twenty to twenty-five, only a relatively few teachers are able to mentor successfully. Equally if not more important and more costly, a faculty person who is expected to mentor students in critical, creative thinking must herself or himself be engaged in such activities. This means that sufficient resources must exist to provide these faculty persons with the time to pursue their own research.

In addition to access to the corpus of accepted knowledge, active engagement in learning, and challenging yet supportive mentoring, critical, creative learning also requires exposure to a variety of different views and methods. This is one reason why, historically, liberal learning has been defined as including the humanities, the physical sciences, and the social sciences. It also explains why many proponents of such learning believe that students need to acquire some facility in, at minimum, one foreign language and ideally spend some time living and traveling in a foreign country. They also feel that students need to be exposed to the arts and to engage in some form of athletic behavior. More recently, supporters of liberal learning have recognized the need to ensure a diverse student body, given the important role played by peers in a student's education and the value of having peers from different backgrounds. Admittedly, student diversity has only become a highly visible issue in recent years, but even forty years ago most liberal arts and science colleges attempted to enroll students from different geographical areas, if not from different ethnic and class groups.

Whatever else these various factors have in common, taken together they constitute an expensive package. Student-faculty ratios need to be kept low and faculty members must be provided with time to pursue not only out-of-the-class supervision but also their own research. It may be possible to save a little here and there by skimping on this and cutting back on that, but the essential ingredient in this type of education remains a low faculty-to-student ratio, which is costly. It may be possible to make the access to knowledge somewhat cheaper by using computer-assisted means. Similarly, some skills, such as language training, may require fewer faculty members if modern audio-visual facilities are available. The essence of this type of education, however—especially the critical thinking component—remains faculty/student interaction, which will never be cheap.

The situation is quite different when we turn to other forms of education. If the goal is primarily to train students to perform specific activities, it may not be necessary to give so much attention to critical, creative thinking. In these cases, the primary needs may be to provide students with access to a specific body of knowledge, give them opportunities to master this material, and develop some means of evaluating how well the students have mastered the material. This can normally be done with a much higher faculty-to-student ratio than the critical, creative form of education. It may even be possible to make greater use of part-time, less costly faculty. In fact, in many cases, especially where practical skills are being taught, it may be more useful to hire professional practitioners as adjunct faculty rather than rely primarily on full-time academics. Another difference is that there may be little need for students to be exposed to different approaches and different views, let alone different cultures and ways of thinking. Similarly, there is no overriding necessity for these students to be provided with any type of extensive education in areas beyond their own fields of expertise, the arts, or athletics. Other students are likely to be helpful as co-learners, especially if there are fewer faculty members around, but the function of such student cohorts in this type of education would not normally require communal living or diversity per se.

There are other cost-related factors that differ for these two types of education. The decision to create and maintain a highly diverse student body requires financial support. In light of the high cost of traditional liberal arts and sciences education and the various ethnic/racial and social class correlations existing in American society, any college or university committed to maintaining a diverse student body must also be willing to provide significant financial aid for a large proportion of its student body. Moreover, it must maintain an aggressive admissions office if it is to solicit the student mix it desires, along with a well-trained and -staffed financial aid office to evaluate the needs of the students and to generate the various financial packages of scholarships, loans, and campus jobs. The need to service a more diverse student body will likely force the institution to offer a greater range of courses. As in most other situations, this is likely to entail additional costs. Equally important, if the institution hopes to maintain the loyalty of its earlier graduates as the composition of the student body changes—and it most definitely needs to if it hopes to solicit the gifts that it requires—it must fund an active and aggressive alumni relations and development office.

While what has been labeled critical, creative education generally costs more than focused, skill-oriented education, the latter form normally entails additional costs of its own. For the most part these costs are related to providing a more extensive institutional infrastructure. While skill-oriented education may require fewer full-time faculty members, a large part-time faculty normally requires more administrators. Similarly, while skill-oriented institutions can rely more heavily on large lectures and access to knowledge through technology, the necessary technological facilities may cost more per student than those required by critical thinking–oriented educational institutions. Since the students are expected to acquire a basic set of core skills, there is also a greater need for standard evaluation procedures, which may convert into higher assessment costs. The additional costs for these items, however, are likely to be significantly less than the those required by a critical, creative education.

It might be argued that I am creating a false dichotomy here. Rather than treating education as two distinct types, higher education should seek to combine them in various ways, ensuring that those primarily interested in receiving a critical, creative education also learn various job-related skills and those primarily interested in acquiring job-related skills also be provided with a meaningful dose of critical, creative education. Unfortunately, while this sounds reasonable and laudatory, it is a path filled with pitfalls. The fact is that each type of education requires quite different techniques and resources. Moreover, students require different types of pre-training and motivation before they can fully benefit from each type. Most liberal education institutions are not prepared to give their students workplace-experience education. In contrast, most business school institutions do not have the faculty to offer a quality liberal arts and sciences education.

There is, of course, clearly another factor involved in this issue, namely, the question of who should attend institutions of higher education. This is a hot political issue that many, if not most, educators try to avoid. As noted earlier, American higher education historically was primarily concerned with educating its future elite. American colleges and universities were expected to produce gentlemen and, to a lesser extent, ladies capable of functioning as members of the clergy, educators, lawyers, physicians, leaders of industry, and so on. As such, institutions of higher education were intended to be selective and to serve as one of the most important gatekeepers of society.

Over the years this situation underwent significant change. With the increased complexities of the economy, more jobs required additional education. In response to this situation, institutions of higher education took on the responsibility of training more people for future employment. As the process continued, access to higher education became a prerequisite for meaningful employment. A college diploma didn't serve as a passport into the American aristocracy but merely as the entry ticket to a well-paid job.[94]

The dilemma, or at least one of the dilemmas, confronting American higher education is that in order to determine what type of educational mix of critical, creative education and technical, employment-oriented education is required, there first needs to be an honest appraisal of the demand for these different types of education.

Other corollary problems are associated with any attempt to combine these two types of education. As noted earlier, the schooling of students is only part of the mission of most institutions of higher education. Many institutions are also expected to generate knowledge and to fulfill various civic responsibilities. Here again, there is often a difference in emphasis, with some institutions being well known for generating what might be called basic research whereas others are expected to be more concerned with providing practical knowledge of varying sorts.[95] Similarly, some institutions serve as a national forum for exploring social and cultural issues, whereas other institutions are involved in concrete community projects. As with the different types of student-focused education, these differences also require different types of resources. Moreover, the cost-to-income ratio also differs. Basic research not only tends to be more expensive than applied research, but for the most part it earns less. Forums often bring national attention, but generally they need to be subsidized. Community work, in contrast, can generate funds if done under contract. In short, as in the earlier situations, the broader, more abstract activities tend to be the more expensive activities.

This same situation holds when it comes to preserving, nurturing, and evaluating knowledge. The more universal and basic the knowledge, the greater the costs and the fewer returns, based upon proprietary rights. While a major liberal education institution, for example, is expected to maintain a complete set of scientific periodicals at considerable cost, it is unlikely to receive any income as a result. On the other hand, a more technically oriented institution can often market its technically relevant knowledge.

While it is theoretically possible to mix these research and civic objectives in different ways with each other and with the different educational objectives discussed earlier, there are clearly certain natural affinities. More specifically, concerns with basic, pure research and with broad social and cultural issues have a natural affinity with each other and with what was described as critical, creative learning, whereas concerns with more applied research, action projects, and technical job-related education have an affinity for each other. The basis of these affinities is not only the inherent specificity of the concerns, but also the types of resources required to pursue these various interests. The former set is inherently more expensive. The expertise required tends to be greater and more expensive to generate. The actual processes entailed and required are likely to extend over a greater period of time, and, in the end, prove economically unproductive.

There are yet two other issues intertwined with those discussed previously that tend to be ignored, or at least averted. The first relates to the question, Who is the primary beneficiary of higher education? The second relates to the question, Who, consequently, should be expected to assume the cost of this education? A general consensus exists that both the individual receiving the education and society benefit, but there is a good deal of disagreement over who benefits most and thus how cost should be allocated. Not surprisingly, this debate overlaps with the discussion regarding what forms higher education should take. The more skill-focused education is commonly defined as serving the individual, because the skills acquired are seen as leading directly to increased income. In contrast, a critical, creative education is often seen as fulfilling social needs even though the long-term benefits to the individual tend to be much greater than those derived from a more technical, skill-oriented education.

It may be argued that there really isn't any clear answer to the questions of who benefits most from higher education or who should be held financially responsible. By and large, I agree. On the other hand, these questions are no more inherently unanswerable than most of the others posed in this chapter. There are, however, no simple answers. What is clear is that without first addressing these questions, we have no hope of generating a rational platform for dealing with the problems we confront.

It should be equally clear to anyone who has followed the various debates that have raged around higher education in recent years that higher education has become a hot political issue. To a large extent, this is perhaps the biggest problem presently confronting higher education. As troubling as the hodgepodge of different programs might be in and of itself, I have little doubt that we could untangle the various issues in an ordered manner if it were not for the associated political implications and agendas. These ideological considerations affect nearly every aspect of the way questions are framed and make it difficult to resolve even fairly simple issues. The first step in bridging these difficulties is to refocus our attention away from the false issues currently dominating the educational debate and toward these real problems.

Other factors also need to be recognized. I refer here to the nearly universal tendency to force higher education institutions into the hierarchical, highly structured organizational mold that pervades modern society and the attempt to impose faulty economic paradigms. In a very real sense, most institutions of higher education in America are voluntary organizations insofar as a great deal of their day-to-day management activities are carried out on a voluntary, collaborative basis. In this respect, most institutions of higher education function more like churches, synagogues, and various communal organizations than they do as business or government corporations and bureaucracies. The ironic twist is that these communal organizations tend to employ market principles to a greater extent than do most corporate organizations, which have historically relied more on hierarchical structures. This is an issue to which we will return. To foreshadow this discussion, the traditional voluntary/market character of higher education would indicate that efforts to impose order and policy from above or externally upon American higher education are likely to fail. Second, however, it would also suggest that there is nothing inherent in American higher education institutions that would make them adverse to utilizing market principles in both the decision-making process and the allocation of resources.

While it can legitimately be argued that the faculty has traditionally been included in nearly all discussions bearing on the character and future of higher education, in one area this has not normally been the case—namely, in regard to financial matters. It is specifically the financial area, however, that needs to be incorporated into the discussion regarding the future of higher education if anything reasonable is to be accomplished. The demands being placed upon higher education are such that it is no longer possible to ignore the financial implications of decisions. Nearly every decision made entails some sort of trade-off. Without the input of an informed faculty, it is futile to attempt to determine what can and cannot be cut. On the other hand, the faculty needs to understand that there are limited resources. Faculty members also must realize that becoming involved in such discussions won't corrupt them. They need not be bound by a neoclassical paradigm in which all programs must be economically self-supporting.

Admittedly, most faculty members would ideally like to function without any financial constraints. Yet we have already seen how expensive education would be without such constraints. It is clear that the American public is not ready to spend over $40,000 per student per year for a quality liberal arts and sciences education for every student graduating from high school. On the other hand, most American are not willing to settle for a higher education that relies almost exclusively on part-time faculty, large classes, and distance learning, even if the cost of such an education is much less. The real question that we need to answer, therefore, is whether there are feasible mixtures.

Can we fashion an educational program that contains a reasonable element of critical, creative learning augmented with less expensive elements that rely more heavily on technological innovations and part-time faculty? Can we maybe even fashion innovative ways of providing critical, creative education that utilize less expensive means than those now seen to be required? Conversely, can we design ways in which students receiving a relatively inexpensive technical education can also be provided with a meaningful exposure to the more traditional liberal arts and sciences education experience without bankrupting the system? These are all legitimate questions, but they cannot be answered in a useful way without input from a fully informed faculty.

As bleak as much of this discussion may appear, there are some indications that the apparently utopian vision just outlined need not remain a dream. In recent years a number of initiatives have been proposed and even implemented that suggest that the type of broad, inclusive discussion and rethinking of our academic priorities and procedures is possible. Admittedly, these initiatives have been greatly outnumbered by the misdirected programs and policies described in chapters 5, 6, and 7. Nevertheless, there is still reason for hope. To move forward, however, we need to tackle the hard questions. Amidst all the conflicting rhetoric dealing with universal education, access for all, educational standards, and societal needs, we need to decide what types of education are required and in what numbers and proportions. We similarly need to honestly price these different types of education. We should calculate not just the costs of the various elements that make up the different types, but the economic and social gains generated by these elements. We should also determine the relative gains for those receiving the education and for society as a whole, in order to determine how the costs can be fairly assigned. We need to learn what works and what doesn't work. All of these questions require a proper framing. As indicated earlier, I would strongly argue that what is required is a pragmatic, flexible market model grounded in the context of American higher education.

9

~

Practical Possibilities
and Successful Innovations

With all of the faulty innovations inflicted upon higher education in recent years noted earlier in this book, there have also been a number of exciting, encouraging signs. None of the problems have been solved, but a few faint paths through the forest appear promising. I have been fortunate to have had the opportunity to travel on a few of these paths. None are paved with gold and all remain full of potholes. Nevertheless, in many cases there does appear to be the proverbial light at the end, and unlike the light at the end of the tunnels being pursued by most, it doesn't seem to be coming from an oncoming freight train. Though these initiatives are interconnected in various ways, I will deal with each one separately to avoid confusing matters more than necessary. I have taken the liberty, however, of including a fair amount of particularistic detail. My purpose in doing so is not to imply that these initiatives need to be implemented exactly in the form presented—this is clearly not the case—but to convey some of the contextual issues that play a role in such initiatives. I should add that since the purpose is merely to indicate some of the types of initiatives that offer promise, a good deal is left out. What they all have in common is a recognition that educational and fiscal issues are interconnected.

RESEARCH MENTORING

One of the more vexing problems confronting higher education that has been touched upon repeatedly in this book and elsewhere is the complex strain generated by the dual expectations that faculty be committed to both teaching and personal scholarship. From an institutional perspective, supporting such personal scholarship in addition to teaching is terribly expensive. On the other hand, given that such personal scholarship is seen as essential to enabling the faculty to imbue their students with an appreciation and facility for critical and creative thinking, it is deemed by most to be a necessity. This expense is exacerbated by the fact that not only must faculty members be provided with the time and resources to pursue their own scholarship, but the ratio of faculty to students must also be maintained at a comparatively low level. The reason is that if the students are to benefit from the faculty expertise generated through the faculty's own research, a highly interactive form of learning is required.

The overall costs of this situation are such that many critics of higher education argue that we need to eliminate, or at least drastically reduce, faculty research and do away with small classes. The only problem with this strategy, of course, is that in the process you will also do away with the type of education that is most highly prized.[96] It should be clear that we are not talking about supporting a research faculty engaged in scholarship unrelated to their teaching responsibilities. This is one of the great misunderstandings that further confuses matters. Faculty members' scholarship and research are not separate from their teaching but central to it. Take away the research and scholarship and faculty members are no longer educational tutors and models; they are reduced to drill instructors.

As counterproductive as this option may be, we need to recognize that the present system isn't working in most places. The strains are just too great. Even the faculty and the students find the situation untenable. The problem is not solely the cost. There is also the issue of the time commitments required. At Queens College, where I teach, increased tuition costs, growing class size, heavier teaching loads, general decreases in public support, and changing demographics have made the situation quite grim. We claim to be a quality liberal education institution, but living up to this claim has become more difficult in recent years, as both faculty and students find it increasingly arduous to meet all of the demands they confront.

With most students working over twenty hours each week to support themselves and increased tuition costs, and the faculty—especially the junior faculty confronting early tenure decisions—pressured to publish, both faculty and students are allocating less and less time to the educational process itself. Many faculty members come onto the campus only two days a week and those who come in more regularly—primarily natural scientists who need their laboratories to do their own work—are often not available to students. This situation not only hurts instruction, but also makes it difficult to provide proper advisement, staff committees, and do all of the other things required to run a healthy, productive educational institution.

Various attempts have been made over the years to change this situation, but the only initiatives that seem to have been successful were extremely expensive since they normally entailed buying back faculty time or providing some other form of monetary incentive. What made this all the more discouraging is that when the resources used to bring about these changes dry up, both student and faculty practices tended to revert back to their prior state.

We had been successful, for example, in carrying out a major curriculum initiative in the area of world studies. This initiative resulted in developing a number of new core courses, including establishing syllabi and training over eighty faculty members to teach them. The classes were kept small—fewer than twenty students, and most were team-taught by two faculty persons from different departments. As one might expect, it was also very expensive since it required providing not only the double released time for two faculty members teaching each course, but also additional released time for the added preparation required. In addition, each faculty participant received a sizable summer stipend. We were able to do this because the program was generously funded through an external grant. Unfortunately, when the money ran out, less than ten faculty members showed any interest in continuing to teach the courses as part of their normal teaching assignments. Without some form of added incentive, they preferred to return to their previous teaching schedules, which were less demanding.[97]

To avoid this sort of problem, we formulated a very different type of program. We called it our Faculty/Student Research Mentoring Program. In brief, it entails releasing faculty members from one of their courses in order to allow them to pursue their own research, if and only if they are also willing to mentor approximately six undergraduate students as research apprentices. In most cases, they are also expected to increase the enrollments in their other classes to make up for the students lost in the course dropped. There are no other incentives offered. As a result, not only is the net faculty cost to the department and college quite low, but there is no attempt to lure unwilling faculty members into the program. Nevertheless, many faculty members vie to participate because the program allows them not only to pursue their own research agenda, but also provides them with some, if minimal, assistance.[98]

Students are likewise recruited in a manner that seeks to build on their perceived self-interests. Few of our students have any pressing intellectual agenda that can be utilized to expand their intellectual horizon. Most want to get a college degree because they believe it will help them get a better job, rather than because it will intellectually empower them. It made little sense, consequently, to offer them greater opportunities for independent study or even more enriched honor-courses as ends in themselves. Doing some extra academic-related work for a faculty member for a stipend, however, is an attractive option since it enables them to cut back, if not eliminate, their part-time jobs, which are less interesting and generally more of a hassle. There is the added plus that in working with a professor, they increase their chances for a good letter of recommendation and may even have the opportunity to acquire specific job skills.

While resources are required to support both faculty and student participants, they are extremely modest by comparison to the funds normally required to solicit such participation. This is due to the fact that in both cases, the activities are built on the existing interests of both parties. The proof of the pudding, as the expression goes, has been in the remarkable success of the program. Begun nearly seven years ago with a modest Ford Foundation Grant and developed later with support from a Department of Education Fund for the Improvement of Post-Secondary Education (FIPSE) grant, the program has recently been institutionalized at the college. Each semester we now offer approximately five grants that support approximately thirty students and five faculty members.

The faculty-support funds come to approximately $2,000 per faculty participant, but even this is probably an exaggeration since participating faculty are normally expected to accept an increased enrollment in their other courses, which will partially offset these costs. The required student funds are drawn from a much larger scholarship pool and amount to less than 3 to 4 percent of the total. Given that the participating students generally acquire useful skills and establish a qualitatively better relationship with a faculty member, nearly all the students acknowledge that they were better off having to put in the additional hours than they would have been by receiving the money without any commitments. We still need to recruit students each semester because they are unaware that the program exists. On the other hand, we continue to receive more faculty proposals than we can fund in any given semester.

The program has had some negative results. Not all projects proved satisfactory to all the participants. A few faculty members took advantage of the system by not fulfilling their part of the bargain. They either failed to pursue the research agenda indicated in their proposal or did not give the students the attention they promised. Given the limited resources expended, however, there were few negative consequences for these failures. We hadn't really given them much, so there wasn't much that could be withdrawn except perhaps the opportunity to participate in similar projects in the future. A number of nonparticipating faculty members were also critical of what they saw as an inherent bias in the program, since it seemed to favor those departments where it was easier to utilize undergraduate assistants. When challenged to come forth with their own projects, however, a good number of these critics did generate proposals of their own and were subsequently funded.

While the program met its initial goals successfully—namely, allowing faculty members to pursue their own scholarship; promoting better faculty/student relationships; providing students with an opportunity to earn needed funds; and fostering greater student involvement in the life of the college—

the unexpected benefits proved to be even more rewarding. To list some of the most important of these:

1. Participating faculty members emerged with a more positive attitude toward the students.
2. Students emerged with not only a more positive attitude toward the faculty, but also with a much more sophisticated understanding about nearly everything related to their education and the college.
3. Meaningful student cohorts were created that served to enhance student learning.
4. New interdepartmental and interdivisional ties were created.
5. Added funding sources were identified and successfully solicited.

The changing faculty attitude toward the students is perhaps best conveyed by the response of one participating faculty member. While this faculty member had a solid research background, he was also one of the more critical members of the faculty when it came to evaluating our changing student body. In submitting his first proposal, he quite openly told me that he had little expectations that the students would be of much help to him. The reduced teaching load and the possibility that the students could do some of the more trivial work made it worth his time to prepare a proposal. It was a strong proposal and it was funded. Three months later, passing by my office, he turned to me and said, "Hey, I didn't tell you, but I really lucked out with the students I got for that project you funded. They're really very good and are doing all sorts of things I didn't think they could do." I said that I was pleased and left it at that.

Two years later, this same faculty member submitted a second Research Mentoring Proposal.[99] Again, it was a solid proposal and it was funded. Two months later, the faculty member came by my office again. "I lucked out again. These new students are even better than the last bunch." This time I couldn't remain silent. "Jack," I said, "Don't you think that maybe it isn't just luck. Maybe these students are simply a lot better than you've previously thought." He stopped, and I could see the wheels spinning. "You know, you're probably right. But how is it that they can function so much better in the research group than they do in class? In class, most of the students seem to be falling asleep. On my research project, they are full of enthusiasm and sharp."

Clearly, a number of factors are involved in what is going on here. In discussing similar situations with various students and faculty members who have participated in one or more of these projects, some points emerge regularly. To begin with, students generally note that the faculty person treats them better. More might be expected of them, but at least the faculty person knows their names. They also report that having the other students around helps them. In a large class, they generally feel lost. Interestingly, those students who have had individual tutorials report that in such one-on-one situations with faculty members, they tend to become intimidated and overwhelmed. A small group working with a faculty member is more effective, as far as they are concerned, since the students can back each other up in all sorts of ways. What one doesn't know or can't do, maybe another can. This, I must admit, was never planned. The reason we established a six-to-one ratio of students to faculty, rather than the one-to-one ratio characteristic of most mentoring programs, was that we didn't have the resources to support a one-to-one program. The fact that our students found the six-to-one ratio more useful was pure serendipity.

The relatively unstructured nature of the research process had its own positive impact. Students were able to exhibit a much wider range of skills and competencies than they could in the normal classroom. In some cases it was language skills. In others it was computer or other technical skills. Given the highly diverse student body at Queens College, other institutions may not have exactly the same experiences that we did. In light of the wide range of experiences and skills characteristic of students in most colleges or universities, however, I would wager that significant student assets go untapped.

There were other unexpected educational benefits. The false starts and mistakes that characterize any research project served to humanize the professor to the students. As one student said to me, "I never realized that professors have to rewrite and rethink their ideas." Up to that time, she claimed she never understood what the professor meant when he or she had urged students to rework their assignments.

Other sorts of traditional stereotypes were toppled. Both the faculty and the students were reminded that knowledge does not always fit into nice departmental or even divisional pigeonholes. As a result, a number of interdepartmental initiatives were undertaken. Equally encouraging from a fiscal and developmental point of view, a significant number of the research mentoring projects funded proved sufficiently productive and interesting to obtain subsequent external support. The most exciting and positive outcome, however, has been the degree to which this program has served to increase the commitment of significant numbers of both faculty members and students to the college and its educational mission.

FINANCIAL MATCHING

The Research Mentoring Program just described is built on an implicit system of matching needs. The faculty wants to pursue its own research; students need part-time jobs; the college wants to increase faculty/student interaction; and so on. While there is nearly always something to be gained by building on complementary needs and interests, the needs and resources of the parties seldom dovetail perfectly. This requires the parties involved to make various compromises. As a consequence, in most situations where resources are plentiful, it is difficult to entice the type of collaboration and give and take that matching generally requires. There is the added problem that such collaboration requires a fairly democratic ethos if it is to work. If one party is in a dominant role, the bargain struck is likely to have been forced upon the subordinate party, with the result that this person's cooperation is likely to be reluctant.

I note these difficulties because they explain why in most organizations, including institutions of higher education, such matching strategies are seldom utilized. All people believe that their needs should be honored and see no reason why they should have to make any sort of additional sacrifices or adjustments to get what they want. Conditions of extreme scarcity change things significantly. Unfortunately, just about the time that resources become sufficiently scarce that people become willing to collaborate, they normally have nothing left to put on the table. The secret to establishing a system of collaboration and matching, therefore, is to provide enough resources to foster an entrepreneurial spirit, but not the sort of sufficiency that leads people to believe they can do what they want on their own.

It also helps if there is a legacy of collaborative, entrepreneurial practices that can be used to legitimate such a system. I would suggest that American higher education, with its inherently voluntary organizational structure, provides such a context. It has also become a place of relative scarcity. Admittedly, my judgment here primarily reflects my own experiences within the City University of New York, which has not only experienced greater economic scarcity in recent years than most other institutions, but also has a history of greater faculty governance. Whether the fairly crude matching system that is about to be described would work as well elsewhere, therefore, is unclear. On the other hand, the underlying conditions it seeks to manage are sufficiently ubiquitous in higher education that I believe it is worth describing.

In 1990, while serving as departmental chair, I was asked to "fill in" as dean of faculty for the social sciences. As things happen in academia, I was there for the next five years. What struck me upon becoming dean was the degree to which the dean's role was similar not only to the chair's role but also to the leadership roles I had held in various community and other voluntary organizations. My main responsibilities were to facilitate the formulation of positions, forge agreements, and encourage cooperation. What is more, I quickly discovered that most of the people I had to deal with looked upon themselves more as volunteers than as employees. My autonomy was further constrained by the fact that coinciding with my tenure as dean, the college underwent a series of severe financial reductions, putting the division in the similar type of *begging* situation I was familiar with from my volunteer days.

Without denying the difficulties and adversities created by what can only be called draconian budget cuts, I am obliged to confess that I found the job to be less onerous than I had expected, especially insofar as it entailed allocating resources. The reason for this was that I created a situation—due in part to financial constraints and in part to my own natural intuition—in which allocation decisions were shared.[100] The process entailed three basic steps.

First, I tried to ensure that all information bearing on available resources, including their sources, was shared with the department chairs. In this context, I wanted them to know not only what resources were available, but also how each department had contributed in earning these resources.

Second, I urged each department and program to think through what their various priorities were and to share this information with me. This, I should note, is not an easy thing for most chairs to do. They may know what their priorities are, but like most middle managers, which is how they function within the institution, they are usually unwilling to share this information. They are unwilling because they fear—often rightly—that resources they label as having a low priority will be taken away without compensating resources being made available for high-priority items. The fact that I guaranteed that they would be informed of all budgetary transactions served to lessen their fears. I further eased their anxiety by telling them that I would make no adjustments among categories without their agreement. In short, not only wouldn't I unilaterally cut their budget in a particular area, but I would also offer an increase to offset any suggested decease. Moreover, I offered to scrap the whole process and return to across-the-board cuts if that was the preference of the majority.

Steps one and two served to make the whole process a more open one. The third step entailed a further pledge on my part to allow transfers between categories for a modest cost. On the surface this may seem like larceny on my part, which in fact it was. Why should a chair be willing, or forced, to give up $10,000 of part-time teaching money to get back $9,000 for computers? The reason, quite simply, is that most organizations make it very difficult to move money from one category to another. This, in turn, is due to the way most budgets are created and managed in higher education.

In higher education, most budgets are based on previous budgets because it generally seems imprudent to go through the arduous and time-consuming process of constructing a new budget each year. The results might be better if we did start fresh each year, but the costs in time and energy would be exorbitant. Consequently, what most chairs and other middle-level managers normally do is attempt to increase their overall budget each year by making a claim that they need more funds in specific categories. If they don't, they are likely to have some categories reduced without any promise of offsetting increases in other categories.

Upper management, for its part, is aware of this situation and therefore makes it very difficult to move money between categories. As a consequence, it is normally hard to move surpluses from one category to another. Given the cost of leaving money unspent in any category—which would result in that category being automatically reduced the next year—these monies are usually spent even when the need is at best modest. Faced with this situation, the option to move money between categories, even for a modest charge, strikes many as quite attractive.

The final step in this process pertains to the way the surpluses, which I acquired, were used. By and large they were set aside as matching funds. Chairs were informed that if they could raise some monies for special projects that would improve their program but were not presently funded, I would attempt to match their contributions. In this way the more aggressive departments were able to recapture the funds that I had been able to free up through the process of exchange noted earlier.

It would be misleading to imply that this system served to alleviate all problems. It didn't. The draconian budget cuts I mentioned were very costly in all sorts of ways. On the other hand, the system did work to mitigate the pain. In a sense, certain departments even felt better off than they had before. This was particularly the case for those departments that either were able to take full advantage of my matching program or were able to use their reallocated resources to increase their own productivity and hence future allocations. While some departments thrived better than others under this system, my own judgment was that by the third year the system was in place, even the most laggard departments had managed to improve their overall financial situations.

The system worked sufficiently well that after three years, it was agreed that I should take a certain percentage of the funds available off the top of my budget to expand the opportunity for such matching. The system had the added benefit of sensitizing all chairs to what our collective priorities were. This was perhaps best exemplified in the decision by the chairs that I provide funds to reduce the teaching loads of newly hired faculty members even while our overall budget was being reduced. I am convinced that without having gone through the types of negotiations we did, in which department chairs had to make a case for their different needs, this would not have happened.

The system produced a number of results that I had not fully anticipated. One was the growth of interdepartmental projects. Because it was easier to move resources about, departments began to feel less protective of their particular pieces of turf. If, for example, a department were receiving some funds to provide a particular service, they would be unlikely to cede that service to another department or even to the division as a whole if this entailed their losing resources. On the other hand, if they could surrender a particular service while still maintaining some of the funds attached to this service by agreeing to expand some other service that they were better equipped to handle, they were more likely to do so. This attitude expressed across departments created a situation in which educationally sound divisional and interdepartmental projects that previously went unfunded became possible. It even made possible various interdivisional arrangements that had previously faltered.

There was another result of this general strategy that to me was perhaps the most significant. I know that some among my colleagues will disagree with me, but I am convinced that the strategy had a significant positive effect on divisional morale. While there was considerable complaining about the comparatively brutal way negotiations were undertaken (I was a hard negotiator), in a sense the process served to empower all the players. While I was the one who clearly set the rules, there were means for others to question them. More important, while I may have set the rules, the decision of how to play or whether to play or not was left to each player.

The process produced two other results that deserve mentioning. The sharing of information and continual negotiations created and demanded an atmosphere of openness and trust that also served to enhance morale. The need to focus attention on one's relative strengths rather than weaknesses had a similar effect. If one wanted to increase resources, it was necessary to focus on one's strength because only in terms of one's strength would one likely get resources. The more common system of demanding more resources to deal with problems was inoperative. As bad as things were— and they were bad—the game forced participants to play up their strengths, not their weaknesses. Call it self-delusion or whatever you like, it served to make people feel better. People tended to see the glass as half-full rather than half-empty.

This matching strategy clearly entails more than money. There needs to be a willingness to share information and a relatively high degree of trust among the parties involved. Another necessary attitude is a willingness on the part of those not directly involved in any particular transaction, implicitly if not explicitly, to sanction such transactions. It could be argued that all parties to the system did so by endorsing the system initially. It is easier, however, to accept an allocation system in the abstract than it is in the concrete. This is especially so when many of the concrete situations entail individuals seeing resources go to others while the common matching pool shrinks. In short, for a matching system like this one to work, everyone has to accept that there is not only an institutional division of labor, but that this division of labor will necessitate a division of resources. Moreover, some parties will have an advantage in obtaining some types of resources and others an advantage in obtaining other types of resources. Everyone hopes that in the long run, resources will be equitably allocated and everyone will come out better, but there is clearly no guarantee.

This matching system and its various offshoots, with all of their limitations, were sufficiently successful that I began to investigate ways of expanding the process to encompass overall institutional planning. I quickly learned that others were wrestling with similar ideas and practices. The specifics varied significantly, but the central themes tended to be similar even if the final decisions were different. The need to rethink how funds were allocated was clearly central. Emphasis was normally also given to examining and relating both the cost and revenue of different programs and activities rather than merely the cost. There was also a concern with establishing ways to integrate financial planning with academic planning. Finally, there was the issue of the role of the faculty and other constituencies in the whole process.

Given the complexity of the problems entailed in any one of these issues, let alone all of them, I realized very quickly that it was highly unlikely that a plan could be crafted that would be acceptable to all. On the other hand, the problem was sufficiently large and the alternatives sufficiently bleak that it was worth the effort to try. While I can't claim the success for the next program that I experienced for the previous two, I would still argue that this method represents an encouraging and potentially rewarding path. In brief, the thesis of this program is that the only way to maintain academic excellence and control costs in American higher education is to integrate institutional financial planning into the faculty governance system along the lines described in the matching program presented here.

TOTAL ACADEMIC AND FINANCIAL PLANNING

It is always difficult to change the way things have historically been done. When the issue is money and the context is one bound by a strong sense of history and tradition—that is, academia—the task is all but impossible. On the other hand, dire circumstances have a way of making the impossible inevitable. Such seems to be the case with financing American higher education. One way or another, things are going to change.

The path, or, more accurately, direction, described in the following example is scary.[101] It points toward uncharted lands. No one—faculty member, administrator, or trustee—is likely to find it attractive. Trustees and administrators tend to distrust the faculty when it comes to financial matters. Most faculty members don't want to have financial responsibilities. The prime motivation for including the faculty consequently remains a dread of what seems to be the only other alternative, namely, greater and more centralized administrative control. For faculty members, it isn't just dread of being stripped of resources, but also the greater dread of losing whatever control they have over these resources. This latter concern is tied to the fact that as resources become scarcer, the administration tends to arrogate unto itself

more and more allocation decisions and to engage in greater micromanagement. This generally leads to administrative growth and increased administrative costs, further exacerbating the scarcity. Perhaps, more destructive is
the fact that such administrative action nearly always generates faculty criticism and a diminishing of institutional morale.

Although this scenario might appear to be acceptable to administrators,
there is much about it that disturbs them as well. While many administrators
might complain about faculty governance, they also realize that it provides
them with a wide range of support. They can share responsibility with the faculty for a wide range of decisions. They are not solely responsible for what
happens. Moreover, most administrators realize that they can't run their institutions by themselves. Neither do they want to incur the added expense of the
type of administrative growth that the abdication of the faculty would require.

Because of these joint concerns, some institutions have attempted to
establish general budgetary formulas and guidelines that can be shared with
the faculty.[102] In addition, some institutions have sought ways of soliciting
faculty and broad institutional collaboration in designing these formulas and
guidelines. Unfortunately, even the best of these programs tends to limit the
role of faculty and departmental control, investing the power instead with
deans and other administrators. The secret in generating a plan that will be
seen as legitimate and that will allow for less administrators rather than more
is to graft resource allocation decisions onto the existing governance system.
No institution with which I am familiar, including my own, has yet been successful in doing this.

While we were not successful in implementing such a plan, and given the
present situation are unlikely to be in the immediate future, we *were* successful in clarifying many of the key elements of such a plan. More specifically, I had the opportunity to chair a committee of faculty and administrative leaders charged with exploring such a possibility for Queens College.
Our *interim* report to the president quite succinctly described the major
problems we encountered and what actions we agreed should be initiated.
It also reveals some of the areas where the parties agreed to disagree.[103]
Clearly, the situation that we faced is different from that faced by many other
institutions. The report speaks in sufficiently general terms, however, that I
believe it is useful to reproduce a slightly edited version here.

The charge to the committee was collaboratively drafted by the president and
some initial committee members. The substantive paragraph reads as follows:

> The committee is charged to examine the present organizational structure of the
> college and to assess innovations and modifications that might serve to
> strengthen the College's academic excellence, further the basic mission of the
> College, and improve economic efficiency. Attention should be given to seek-
> ing means for reducing administration overhead wherever possible and increas-

ing departmental and faculty responsibilities in fiscal matters related to the academic offering of the College. In this context, the Committee should articulate ways to improve departmental management and to make departments and other academic units sensitive to the budgetary constraints within which the College must operate. The Committee should feel free to review a wide range of practices and possibilities, including those bearing on departmental and divisional structures, alternative pedagogies, auxiliary services, fundraising, academic and nonacademic staffing customs, and student and faculty recruitment.

After identifying the committee members, outlining the procedures, and listing groups and individuals consulted, the report presented a brief synopsis of the basic challenge we confronted, the guiding principles we agreed upon, and our basic recommendations. They were as follows:

The Challenge

The issues and objectives outlined in the Charge presented above are directly related to the many challenges, including financial cutbacks, confronting higher education, especially public higher education. While costs continue to increase due to inflation and an overall growth in higher education, public support has decreased. Public higher education is expected today to do more with less, and this trend is likely to continue if not intensify. Faced with this situation, institutions of higher education have attempted in recent years to improve their overall economic efficiency by imposing stricter management procedures. Unfortunately, few institutions of higher education have historically possessed the management structure required to benefit from such procedures. This has resulted in administrative growth, which has commonly cost more than any savings generated within the ranks. As this situation has become more and more apparent, educational administrators have been forced to consider radical solutions to their problems. To generate savings needed, they now seem to be contemplating drastically restructuring the academy rather than merely seeking out marginal efficiencies. More specifically, they are experimenting with increasing the numbers of cheaper part-time faculty, enlarging class size, relying more on what is hoped will be less expensive technological techniques, and reconfiguring what students will receive. While faculties across the country have by and large responded negatively to these trends, they have often failed to suggest alternative remedies. In response to such faculty challenges, serious arguments have been proposed for decreasing faculty governance powers by eliminating tenure and making departmental chairs, deans and other administrators more responsive to senior administration and nonacademic boards by means of top-down appointments.

While the call for increased funding of higher education must be supported, political and financial reality requires that something quite radical be done if public institutions of higher education are to survive. *It is important, however, that all such changes serve to maintain and further enhance the overall educational process and product.* This requires understanding and respecting differences among different educational institutions and different academic programs offered by such institutions. More concretely, what constitutes both optimal and acceptable class size, reliance upon adjunct teachers, and use of computers and multimedia technology varies from institution to institution and department to department. While academic departments in every college in the country suffer from some economic and academic inefficiencies, they can normally best be corrected by the faculty within these departments. The crucial question is how.

Guiding Principles

Based on its deliberations and consultations, the Committee believes that the most effective solution is for the faculty to participate more fully in managerial and financial College issues. For this to occur, a number of things are required. Perhaps the most important of these is the willingness of the faculty to assume this responsibility. While this represents a very real challenge to any institution of higher learning, Queens College is fortunate in having a lengthy tradition of active faculty participation in many forms of college governance. The rights and responsibilities of the faculty are embedded in the existing governance structure which gives the faculty, through its Personnel and Budget (P & B) Committee, extensive rights and responsibilities over personnel and budget issues. While the faculty has historically exercised these rights and responsibilities regarding personnel matters, it has not done so to the same degree regarding budget matters. The recent establishment by the College P & B Committee of a subcommittee on budget to mirror its subcommittee on personnel (Committee of Six), however, indicates a willingness to assume greater budgetary responsibility. The various discussions held by this Committee noted above have similarly indicated a widespread willingness to accept such responsibility.

For the faculty to assume greater budgetary responsibility, more is required than simply the willingness to do so. The Committee's deliberations and discussions identified eight key issues that need to be addressed:

1. Need to increase faculty/departmental involvement in long-term financial planning;
2. Need to limit administrative growth;
3. Need to enhance administrative support;
4. Need to balance economic, academic, and other criteria;
5. Need to ensure flexibility for growth and experimentation;
6. Need to increase transparency of budgetary and allocative processes;
7. Need to work within and improve the existing governance structures; and
8. Need to improve the collaboration between administration and faculty.

While some of these issues can begin to be addressed immediately, others will require further deliberation before specific recommendations can be made. Since there is overlap among many of these items, our recommendations deal with them concurrently.

Recommendations

I. The Administration should establish mechanisms for more extensive sharing of administrative and budgetary information and policies with

departmental Personnel and Budget (P & B) Committees and other appropriate College constituencies.

The Committee recommends that a series of workshops be established during the spring semester to begin this process. In keeping with the goal of creating an ongoing structure capable of not only contributing to the more efficient management of the College, but a structure capable of modifying itself, the Committee believes that the participants in these workshops should be able to organize their own activities, structure, and membership as much as possible. The Committee does believe, however, that initially these workshops must minimally familiarize departmental P & B committees with the various funding and allocative models presently in use. These should include the models used last year by both the Restructuring Committee and the Academic Priorities Committee, which have been further modified by members of this Committee, and the Adjunct Allocation Model recently revised by the Provost. A steering committee made up of representatives from the Provost's Office, the College P & B, and this Committee should be charged with initiating such workshops during the spring semester. It is the intention of this Committee that these workshops evolve into enduring mechanisms capable of discussing, analyzing and contributing to the solution of a wide range of administrative and organizational concerns. It is also our intention that they serve as a prototype for examining the practical details required to implement new initiatives noted below.

II. The Administration should work to implement broadened fiscal governance.

In keeping with the general objective of making fiscal management a more democratic and open process, it is important that the proper and necessary mechanism be established to advise the President in these matters. This requires developing procedures not only for making decisions, but also for reviewing the criteria and assumptions entailed in these decisions. Guidelines and procedures for managing budgetary matters should be established similar to those now utilized for managing academic personnel matters. The Committee recognizes that this will require a great deal of effort on the part of the entire College community.

The Committee believes that it is also important to recognize student interests and needs when determining allocations. This is particularly important when funding services such as registration, advisement, counseling, library services, and club activities. The Committee recommends that the Dean of Student's Office and the Office of Academic Advising undertake a survey of students' needs and preferences to guide this process.

The Committee believes that the Provost in consultation with the appropriate Deans should begin to explore the possibility of entering into multi-year overall departmental plans. These agreements should be based on the College's and department's long-term academic priorities and overall financial situation. The objective would be to set specific academic and budgetary objectives in accordance with guidelines and principles articulated in the workshops noted above. Within these guidelines, departments would be given greater flexibility in allocating their resources. Such arrangements would both provide the workshops with concrete experimental models and serve as paradigms for adoption by other departments.

If departments are to do more than survive, they also need to have an opportunity to undertake various types of initiatives. Such initiatives require resources. The Committee, therefore, recommends that the Provost's Office in collaboration with the College P & B explore options, especially as part of any departmental agreement, for establishing dedicated funds for special initiatives by departments or other academic clusters. While details of such a program require further study, there was considerable sentiment within the Committee in favor of setting aside funds from the Provost's Office to complement funds set aside for particular innovations by departments.

III. The Administrative structure and procedures should be reviewed with the goal of incorporating the new faculty role most effectively.

Given the increased responsibility that each department will have for its own management, questions arise regarding the type of administrative structure and support likely to be most practical. There is clearly an expectation that increased departmental fiscal responsibility would be accompanied by a more streamlined administration, which would support departmental decision making and provide the information required to facilitate the process. This raises the issue of the most efficient administrative structure. Some options were noted in preliminary Committee discussion, including: (1) maintaining the present system as is; (2) retaining the present structure but adding specific college-wide responsibilities to those already assigned to divisional deans; and (3) replacing the present divisional structure with a more functional alternative, such as: a dean for faculty administration who would oversee departmental budgetary items—such things as adjunct allocation, workloads, OTPS expenditures, etc.—to ensure that each department was in conformity with its own budget; a dean for curriculum matters who would oversee curriculum matters, including various interdepartmental and interdivisional programs; a dean for research and external relations. In conjunction with any of these options, it would also be possible to allocate to designated chairs specific divisional responsibilities now assumed by divisional deans. While the Committee believes that these matters are of central importance, it strongly feels that further discussion of these and other options is required before it can make any recommendations. Whatever the final structure adopted, the underlying assumption is that the resulting administration would be as lean as possible.

IV. During the next two to three years, there should be an effort to restrict executive pay and REM-level positions.

While the Committee is unable at this time to make any specific recommendations regarding either the appropriate administrative structure, size, or cost, it does believe that the number of higher level administrative positions be limited. As indicated earlier, the size and cost of higher education administration—nationally and locally—has grown during the last few decades. Queens College currently has eleven individuals serving on Executive Pay lines. This represents a decrease of two in the last year. This is not a particularly large number in view of the College's complexity and its reporting responsibilities to CUNY central. The first priority, however, as budgets shrink, must be to get funds to the classroom to serve our students. To that end, efforts to curb the growth of higher-level administrative staff is critical.

The report recommends that a number of concrete steps be taken. Some were taken, including a two-day workshop for all departmental chairs. At this workshop, practically all available financial information bearing on the amounts and sources of all income and all allocations were shared. In addition, various allocation models were discussed and examined. As predicted by the committee, approximately one-third of the faculty leaders responded with enthusiasm and claimed to be willing to assume greater fiscal responsibility for their units if provided with the necessary support in return for greater autonomy. Approximately one-third responded quite differently, indicating that they were already overworked and they feared being blamed for future cuts. The other third remained indecisive.

The faculty response points out one of the more ironic aspects of this entire process. If fiscal and academic issues are to be more closely linked in a manner that preserves the existing faculty governance structures, academic administrations will have to take the lead. Without the active cooperation of the faculty in setting allocative priorities, however, academic administrations will be forced to grow exponentially and even then they are likely to fail. Unfortunately, both the faculty and the administration find themselves in what is referred to as a prisoners' dilemma situation.[104] If each group acts to maximize its own utility, they will both end up in a worse situation than if they cooperated. Unfortunately, cooperation requires a relatively high degree of mutual trust and this trust is rapidly eroding.

While I must admit to being more pessimistic than I was ten years ago, I remain enough of a rationalist to believe that reason might yet prevail. More important, there is nothing that complex about either the correct diagnosis or cure. The central problem confronting American higher education is not any of those detailed in chapters 1 and 3. Consequently, the cures described in chapters 5, 6, and 7 are more destructive than helpful. The problem is rather the very simple, but still very painful, one of trying to do too much with too little.

We need first to recognize what different types of education cost. I have tried to show that traditional liberal education is an extremely expensive product. Admittedly, other forms of education are cheaper, but there is no way to deliver the expensive version for the cost of the cheaper versions. This is not to deny that there can be cost-control measures even in the case of the most expensive versions. Such measures, however, are best built into the existing control system, which means into the existing joint faculty/administrative governance system, rather than externally imposed. In utilizing the existing faculty governance system, it is important not only to make use of the expertise of faculty members but also to be sensitive to their interests and needs. At the same time, we need to determine what we are willing to pay and how these costs are to be allocated. Here again, we need to realistically assess the resources, needs, and interests of the various parties, be they students, parents, potential employers, trustees, alumni, taxpayers, or interested observers.

The promise of the three initiatives described in this chapter is that through a mixture of planning and happenstance, they build on the self-interests of the various participants. As such, all three recognize and respect the inherently volunteer nature of most institutions of higher education. They similarly recognize and respect that these institutions are living in a period of scarcity that is likely to continue. All three initiatives also implicitly, if not explicitly, acknowledge that the greatest resources available to all institutions of higher education are the energy and commitment of their faculty and students. Grants and gifts are lovely, but only the largest of either can compare to the net gain that a moderately more committed and dedicated faculty and student body brings to an institution.

Another factor that informs all three initiatives is the fact that each is essentially about process rather than content. Each embodies a way of doing something rather than specifying what should be done. Each also represents a means whereby new growth can be derived from apparently barren resources. In the American situation this growth has historically embraced not only the individual students being educated, but also American society itself. I would suggest that it is this fundamental commitment to disciplined change and growth embodied in the ideals of both American society and its institutions of higher education that explains the very special role higher education has historically played in America.

Whatever honorific position higher education may have once held in America, it would appear that this is no longer the case. In part, this loss of faith has been due to some of the perceived problems and difficulties that have plagued higher education during the last few decades. There is also a sense, however, that the problem lies with a loss of faith in the American ideals of opportunity, democratic communities, and respect for differences.

It is here that we confront a major paradox reflected in the title of this study, which somehow underlies this whole discussion. I would describe it as the incongruity of the flexibility and social character of real markets versus the rigidity and self-maximizing character of the dominant neoclassical market paradigm. As I have argued in other contexts, markets and market thinking need not be feared; what we should fear is a grossly distorted view of how markets function.[105] It is exactly this type of misunderstanding that underlies not only most of the counterproductive actions recommended by educational critics, but also the failure of so many faculty members to accept fiscal responsibility for their own institutions. It is still possible, I believe, for these trends to be reversed and for there to be a renewed appreciation of what American institutions of higher education have been and can yet be. Such a renewed appreciation would also serve to help us recapture our faith in the American dream.

10

～

Recapturing the American Dream

The central theme of this book has been that the real plight of American higher education lies in a widespread and pervading tendency, first, to misread its fiscal and organizational reality and then to recommend and impose counterproductive changes. The reality, for example, is that the costs of higher education, given inflation and changing expectations, despite claims to the contrary, have been reasonable and justified. Admittedly, there has been an exponential increase in tuition costs, but this has been due primarily to a transfer of costs previously funded from other sources to tuition. In short, while higher education has been subject to severe economic criticisms, the critics by and large have been wrongheaded.

Most complaints and criticisms concerning the way higher education institutions have historically been managed are similarly misguided. Rather than being a highly wasteful system full of all sorts of irrational and inefficient practices such as tenure, sabbatical leaves, and unnecessary research, higher education has produced an efficient, inexpensive governance system appropriate for its particular needs. It could be argued, in fact, that present restructuring within the corporate world that emphasizes decentralization, less hierarchical structures, greater teamwork, and leaner administrative structures are mimicking traditional academic structures.

Admittedly, there are real problems. The great majority of these, however, are a direct result of faulty efforts to change the way things have traditionally been done. Moreover, most other problems are due to a large extent to the fixation on these wrong issues. This hinders our ability to deal with the real problems in a rational, constructive manner. This fixation also serves to undermine a number of initiatives that might serve to correct existing deficiencies and put us on a more promising path.

Something more seems to be going on here, however, as I noted at the end of chapter 9. In attempting to force higher education into the hierarchical organizational mold characteristic of most corporate structures, the critics have only succeeded in convincing many faculty members that they are best served by avoiding fiscal issues. At the same time, we seem to have lost sight of what American higher education was intended to be. Fashioned in the light of the American dream itself, American higher education was intended to be both inclusive and diverse. This is not to deny its important historical gatekeeping role or its more practical training role. There need not be any contradiction here since American higher education was not committed to a single canon or a single process. If American higher education is to maintain the prestigious international reputation it has earned over the years, it needs to maintain this rich diversity. Rather than attempt to create a homogeneous hodgepodge, it needs to recognize and accept diversity.

The true glory of American higher education is that it managed to combine the prestige of the Ivy League with the hope of public night colleges; the idealistic, ivory tower mentality of the academy and the practical concerns of technical colleges. As such, American higher education has been a remarkable and successful social experiment. We need to build on its successes and learn from its failures, rather than attempt to make it conform to the dictates and needs of other institutions. This requires not so much attempting to replicate its past deeds but rather understanding and honoring the principles that made it work. I have already touched upon most of these principles in passing. In this final chapter, I shall focus upon them more explicitly.

American higher education is varied. No set mold exists into which all institutions must fit. American higher education institutions vary dramatically in size, with some numbering only a few hundred students whereas others serve 10,000, 20,000, or over 40,000 students. Some are single sexed; others are coeducational. The students on certain campuses tend to be homogeneous in age, race, and ethnicity. On other campuses, diversity is the rule. Some institutions have expansive campuses that are dotted with dorms, classroom buildings, laboratories, athletic facilities, and even hotels and stores. Others have no real campus, surviving in rented buildings scattered in metropolitan areas. The curriculum at some institutions is highly determined, with nearly all students taking the same courses in the same order. At other institutions each student selects from numerous different courses, and seldom do any two students end up taking the same set of courses.

The types of courses students take also vary greatly, as does the way these courses are conducted. Some courses are based primarily on what might be called classical readings and focus on abstract ideas and issues; others are highly instrumental and are concerned with training students in a particular skill or vocation. Some course are taught in large lectures, whereas others are taught in small groups or even in one-on-one situations. Some courses are taught by professors with many years of experience and many publications to their credit, while others are taught by part-time instructors or senior students. In some courses and/or institutions, students are expected to read prodigious amounts of material and write extensively, whereas in other courses and/or institutions students read little and write less.

Not surprisingly, these highly varied offerings produce highly varied results. This, in turn, has prompted a number of critics to call for greater consistency, reinforced by established academic standards. What these critics fail to understand is that these differences exist in order to serve different ends. One of the great strengths of American higher education is that it did not evolve to serve a single end but to serve a multitude of ends. It is a system that allows some students to pursue practical ends whereas others are able to develop their abilities for more abstract thought and rumination.

These differences evolved not only to serve different ends, but also to utilize different resources. As such, they vary considerably in expense. Some types require not only a significant commitment of time and energy on the part of the students, but also similar commitments from faculty and staff as well as extensive material support. Other types can be provided with considerably fewer resources and, consequently, cost much less.

The goal should not be to find a single form of higher education to cover all situations, but to evaluate the different needs that exist and to fashion appropriate means for meeting these needs. This means respecting differences, not trying to obliterate them. It also means determining what goes with what and seeking the best and most efficient procedures and practices for delivering the type of education and training required. Here again, there is unlikely to be any single answer. There are ways of mixing vocational training with the liberal arts and sciences.

Similarly, there are ways of combining small classes and mentoring situations with large lectures and distance learning. The central point is that there is no general rule on how this should be done. We need to experiment with various mixes in response to both the needs and resources that exist. If something can be done as well differently and more cheaply, fine; on the other hand, if something needs to be done a particular way and there is a pressing need to do it, the necessary resources must be found. Through all of this deliberation and review, it is equally important to determine who needs what. Not everyone is suited to be a physician. On the other hand, society needs a certain minimum number of these professionals just as much as it may find it difficult to support a surplus. The same situation holds for schoolteachers, engineers, lawyers, and business consultants.

In arguing for educational diversity, I am not disregarding academic standards. We need standards, no matter what the curriculum and what the objective. Unfortunately, standards, like set curricula, are often used as a means for forcing everyone into a given mold rather than as a means of ensuring excellence. An older generation, when confronted with a younger generation that is unfamiliar with the ideas and texts with which the "elders" grew up, is apt to react critically and even angrily. There is much that such a younger generation is likely to know, however, with which the older generation is unfamiliar.

In some cases, generally those where these differences reflect changing technology, the older generation is apt to take these transitions in stride. When it comes to literary classics and historical and cultural texts, however, such transitions are likely to be contested. It isn't a question, therefore, of whether there should be standards. Nearly everyone agrees that there should be. The question really is how these standards are to be established. Experience would seem to indicate that when it comes to higher education, as in most all other areas, the best standards are those that ensure that people who meet the standards will be able to function satisfactorily in the designated practices. In the context of American higher education, while this will normally entail some input from future employers, students, parents, and even trustees and politicians, the most important input is likely to come from the faculty members who are deemed to be experts in the particular practice. Obviously, the faculty should not operate by decree in these matters. There should be an opportunity for all interested parties to participate.[106] Even without such nonfaculty input, however, there will be heated debate because any faculty worth its salt is a mixed faculty with mixed opinions. We have already seen this. It is such differences of opinion that make a consensus on issues so difficult to achieve.

Change and debate do not just characterize higher education. To a large extent, they constitute the substance of higher education, especially traditional liberal arts and sciences education. This is not to deny the important role played by classical texts and materials. One of the major goals of a good liberal education, however, is to enable students to deal with different perspectives and how these perspectives are affected by a changing world. The great classics have an ability to reveal to us how basic human situations have been experienced by others in other times. The goal, or at least one of the goals, of liberal education is to enable students to appreciate the similarities of very different situations, as well as the differences among apparently similar situations. Such knowledge is inherently empowering. It enables students to confront, evaluate, and even master new situations. It teaches them not merely how to answer particular questions but, more important, how to question new situations intelligently.

Learning how to question intelligently is perhaps the hallmark of American higher education. Few American students have ever been able to compete with comparatively similar students from foreign countries when it comes to factual knowledge and computational skills. Similarly, they often lack both the written and oral skills that many foreign students possess. Where they have historically shone, however, has been in their ability to think creatively and critically about a wide range of issues.[107] This is true not only of those receiving a liberal arts and science education, but of those receiving a more focused vocational education.

The ability to question is closely related to another facet of American higher education. American higher education is intended to be a beginning, not an end. To be an educated person means to be a person who has the ability to continue to learn. This explains, I think, why nearly all American colleges and universities award degrees. As pointed out in a footnote earlier, degrees are intended to be what their name indicates, namely, stages in a lifelong enterprise. Diplomas, which are more commonly awarded in other countries, in contrast, signify an official, often governmental, acknowledgment of having accomplished something or having attained a particular status.[108] This ongoing facet of American higher education is reflected in the number of older Americans who continue to pursue their education, either by taking evening courses or by attempting to earn degrees years after the age when most of their cohorts had done so. It also serves, of course, to add to the diversity and mix that make up American higher education.

The extent to which older Americans are engaged in higher education touches upon another issue of some importance, namely, the question of whom higher education is meant to serve. Is it there to meet the needs of individuals or is it there to serve various social needs? An obvious corollary of this question is, Whose responsibility is it to fund this education? The answer to the first question is quite simple. Higher education is intended to serve both the individuals involved and the larger society. The answer to the second would thus likewise seem to be simple. The responsibility for funding education should reside with both the individuals attending and the larger society.

There are other questions, however, to be asked, if not answered. Should students be solely responsible for their share of their educational costs, or should parents be expected to contribute? Should society's share be paid out of general taxes or should some forms of future tax credit be established? Should certain types of education receive more societal support than others receive? A whole range of such questions deserve attention.

The question of who shall pay what for what has become the key question bearing on American higher education. It is this concern that has spawned a good deal of the other concerns that presently plague higher education. Admittedly, a number of critics out there are angry about what is being taught as well as how it is being taught. Yet others are indignant over who is being educated. It is generally only when these criticisms and concerns are linked to the cost of education and how this cost is allocated to the public at large, that such criticism gains wide recognition. No one seemed to worry too much about college boys spending their time eating goldfish and squeezing into telephone booths when the parents of these boys, or the institution itself, were assumed to be paying the bills. When the state is picking up a significant percentage of the bill, however, suddenly everyone is interested in students' reading comprehension and television habits.

Although the dual responsibilities of higher education creates conflict over who owes whom, there is significant value to the debate. For one thing, if the issues are properly formulated, they can raise important issues and serious discussion can occur. I have already noted most of these issues, but they are worth repeating since they are often lost in debates about false issues.

What types of education should be offered? Liberal arts and sciences, technical, agricultural, business, civic, or any of a number of other alternatives?

If more than one type, what should the mix be?

Who should get what type and what type of prerequisites should be required?

What pedagogical techniques should be used in each case?

How should the costs in each case be allocated?

I have already indicated my own preferences in each case. I believe we should seek diversity in what we offer. We need to determine which methods and resources are required of these various types and then seek to put programs together that have some sort of internal synergy. I have also indicated that these decisions require the active participation of the experts responsible for delivering these products, which in nearly every instance means the relevant faculty.

The question of who should receive what type of education is an entirely different matter that should not be left to academics. In the best of all possible worlds, all types of education would be made available to everyone throughout his or her lifetime. Unfortunately, as I have shown, most education is very expensive. Most people can't afford even a basic liberal arts and science education, let alone a lifetime worth of education. Even less expensive forms of education require significant types of support.

As in most situations where resources are lacking, I would suggest that the principle of matching be utilized. This, of course, is what we have done knowingly and unknowingly for generations. The process needs to be made more transparent, however. Most people, for example, don't realize that a student paying full tuition at practically any Ivy League or equivalent college receives a greater hidden stipend from his or her college than the present tax support received by students attending many, if not most, state colleges and universities.[109]

There is similarly little general knowledge regarding what resources are expended to support different types of academic programs within the same college or university. Obviously, there will be differences and it makes little educational sense to attempt to make everyone survive on the same budget. As in any enterprise, however, it is important to know what costs what and from where resources are coming. Only when this information is known and factored into the educational needs and priorities can rational decisions be made regarding which program may need to be reduced and which one expanded.

Similar types of information are needed before we can make rational decisions regarding how overall costs should be allocated. We know quite clearly that a person with a college education earns on average a considerably higher income than does someone without such an education. We also know as a consequence that a college-educated person pays more taxes than does someone without a college education. A university professor, however, is unlikely to earn as much as a successful lawyer or physician. It isn't simply a matter of professions. A schoolteacher working in the inner city of most major metropolitan areas is likely to earn considerably less than his or her classmate who ends up teaching in a wealthy suburb. Even the inner-city teacher is likely to earn more than a classmate who elects to become a freelance sculptor.

Here again, there are various ways in which this issue can be approached. Some are already, or have in the past been, in use. The military offers scholarships in return for a commitment to serve in the armed forces for a number of years. Some states have offered tuition forgiveness for students willing to go into certain professions. Others have suggested a formula whereby students should be responsible for a certain percentage of their educational costs and the state another percentage. There are long-term borrowing plans as well as prepaid plans. Unfortunately, few if any of these plans are based on any sort of rigorous evaluation of the true costs and benefits of the education offered. As a result, we have students going into social work and teaching with student loans five times greater than they can expect to earn in a year. Other students on scholarships emerge with little or no loans and go on to earn to earn hundred of thousands of dollars a year on Wall Street. I am not sure what the answer is to these inequities, but with income differentials between those with and without a college education increasing and state educational budgets skyrocketing while support per student decreases, the present situation cannot continue for long. American higher education has been part of America's pride. Today, it is one of its major problems. It requires a communal solution.

It is appropriate that we seek such a communal solution, because education is itself an inherently communal activity. It is, in many ways, a community of communities: undergraduate students, graduate students, faculty, staff, administrators, trustees, alumni, parents, and friends, with each of these groups made up of smaller communities. It has also been a highly democratic community, dependent upon a volunteeristic governance system. Parents and family might create pressures and the job market might exert its own force, but unlike in elementary school, students attend college voluntarily. Their teachers similarly have to make very specific decisions before they end up on a college faculty, as do trustees and administrators. More to the point, appointment and/or election to particular leadership positions, especially within the faculty, require that the person be willing to serve, often for little or no financial remuneration.

It is specifically this voluntary governance structure that enables most colleges and universities to function without the cost and the large administrative structures characteristic of other organizations of similar size. Unfortunately, this voluntary governance structure has also emerged as the primary target of so many critics of higher education, including many internal critics. It's disappointing and somewhat comical to see presidents and chancellors, coming from the business world and earning anywhere from five to ten times what the average faculty member earns, rant and rave about tenure, sabbatical leaves, the lack of merit pay, and faculty governance. With equally naïve business and political leaders urging them on, they advocate a slash-and-burn policy that undermines their own institutions. No one would deny that free riders exist among any faculty, but they are seldom, if ever, weeded out by these attacks. The true victim is normally institutional morale, which leads to increased institutional apathy, alienation, and greater inefficiencies.

Existing governance structures are not without their faults. As a group, faculty members tend to resist dramatic, and even undramatic, change. More often than not, however, their hesitation proves to be justified. Moreover, whatever its drawbacks this system is remarkably inexpensive. Any institution that could eliminate 90 percent of its managerial costs overnight and still function pretty much as it did previously would, I believe, jump at the opportunity. The savings would more than cover any additional expenses incurred by the loss of the previous managerial structure. Unfortunately, in the case of higher education, administrators are in the process of building such a managerial structure, with all the costs entailed, with little to no prospect of generating any sort of offsetting savings. In fact, such administrative growth tends to be doubly inefficient, as it serves to frustrate the normal initiatives that tend to flourish in highly unstructured environments.

Good things often have been accomplished even when the forces behind them have been slight, for the simple reason that no major resistance was encountered. A professor initiates a new course built around her most recent research. Two chairs establish an interdisciplinary course to service some of their joint majors. Students organize a group to feed the homeless. A group of drama and music faculty and students organize a free concert in which new works are played. And so on. These types of events are the lifeblood of many institutions. Unfortunately, with the increase in associate and assistant deans and provosts and the red tape they generate, such initiatives run into more and more hurdles, leading to a greater hesitancy on the part of their backers to even try something new.

Here we return to a lesson that we have encountered before, namely, the potential and value of an open, free, unstructured educational environment. Obviously, like anything else, too much freedom and too little structure are apt to be counterproductive in higher education or anywhere else, for that matter. On the other hand, if there ever were a place where the opportunity to think, feel, and act differently needs to be encouraged, it is in our institutions of higher education. Both students and faculty need to be empowered to be somewhat irresponsible. There will always be plenty of opportunities and situations for both groups to conform to others' expectation and march in step. I realize that many critics would argue that the problem with higher education, like the problem with the world in general, is too little order. Even a cursory review of human history, I would suggest, reveals quite the opposite. True believers and autocratic, authoritarian individuals and regimes have been the source of considerably more pain and destruction than dreamers and eccentrics.

Admittedly, the imported carping business leaders are not the first autocrats to inhabit academia. For generations, institutions of higher education have been the home of many autocratic leaders. The main difference between the old autocrats and many of today's is that before, they normally came out of the faculty. They may not have been dreamers themselves, but most understood and valued the dreamers. They usually shared the same basic values of the faculty. Moreover, they understood what faculty governance was all about. They were often bullies and tried to move the faculty in specific directions, but they accepted and respected the inherent rights of the faculty. Many of today's autocrats don't even understand what faculty governance entails, let alone accept and respect it.

What makes most recent faculty- and institution-bashing by politicians and imported business leaders so painful is that even while they assume the right to remake these institutions into what they desire, they refuse to acknowledge their own proprietary responsibilities. In contrast to Theodore White's observation, noted earlier, that education was America's welfare system, many of these critics now seem to treat higher education, especially public higher education, as part of our welfare system. As such, they want it cut and diminished or, at minimum, they want public spending for it lessened. If they acknowledged their ownership, they might begin by looking for the strengths and values present. They might then avoid the cheap shots that are the mark of so many critics. They would begin to treat these institutions not as means to other ends but as valuable assets in their own right.

My call, or perhaps more accurately, my cry, that higher education cease to be the target of ill-conceived attacks, is not directed at one or another specific political group. Enough silly things have been said in recent years to spread the onus around. Admittedly, most of the attacks on faculty governance and assumed abandonment of the classics have come from the political right. Attacks on the irrelevancy of curricula, loss of moral teachings, criticisms of assumed economic and managerial inefficiencies, and assumed loss of standards, however, have come from all political directions. The irony of this is that higher education was at one time the darling of both the political left and right. If America was celebrated as a land of opportunity, higher education was seen as the means toward this opportunity. It still is. Both the political left and right owe it their support.

Amidst all of the other particulars discussed in this book, one important aspect of higher education has been slighted. Higher education can be and should be joyful. Nowhere else can one find the rich trove of ideas, experiences, and opportunities that are to be found on even a modestly endowed academic campus. Colleges and universities are places made for growth. They are institutions that are designed to empower their tenants, be they students or faculty. One can find not only pictorial and sculptured masterpieces to peruse and music to listen to, but the occasion to engage in these activities with the guidance of professional practitioners. There are literary classics in numerous languages to read and new worlds to explore. There are also old and new games to play at various levels of proficiency and lifelong friends to make. In colleges and universities, one can allow oneself to be swallowed up in unique and exciting experiences while at the same time empowering oneself to follow one's own path. They are places for reflection and places to experiment with action. One can become one's own person and discover how to live with others. All of these things bring with them certain anxieties, but insofar as they represent the nectar of life, the overriding experience is one of joy.

We have many reasons to believe that our higher educational institutions may well prove to be valuable models for other institutions in the future. Brief reference was made to the governance needs of symphony orchestras. In other emerging organizations, there is a similar need to both respect the professional autonomy of employees yet ensure economic and managerial efficiency. This is clearly happening in the medical area, where there is an increased resistance to a similar type of hierarchical management being imposed on physicians by HMOs. What they reject is the hierarchical organizational structure common to most for-profit HMO business organizations. Moreover, as in higher education, attempts to impose such hierarchical structures upon them tend to be counterproductive in the long run. There is reason to believe that higher education, and more specifically the historical governance system of higher education if it can be modified to respond properly to economic factors, may prove to be a valuable model for these other fields.

This situation has a highly ironic aspect. In criticizing higher education for its fiscal and organizational intransigence, critics have regularly pointed to the lack of hierarchy, open structure, tolerance, flexibility, and permissive character of the academy. These, of course, are exactly the same characteristics that the same critics and others often praise when defending markets and a market philosophy in other spheres. It is specifically such a grounded market approach that represents the major promise for American higher education. In contrast, the primitive, pay-as-you-go, cut-costs-and-increase-revenue models that are so often proposed represent pitfalls to be avoided. They only serve to obfuscate the real problems and issues and to alienate the goodwill and efforts of faculty and others who are needed to solve the very real problems we confront.

In closing, therefore, I would like to urge everyone to become more involved in American higher education. Become conversant with the issues that are under discussion and debate at those institutions that are in your community or with which you have some sort of relationship. Find out the type of financial support that your state is providing for public education and how it compares with past support and the support offered by other states. Be a critical listener when presented with the false diagnoses and faulty cures that are so freely bandied about these days. I hope some of the facts, figures, and stories contained in this book will help.

Appendix

Methodological Note: An Outsider's Inside View

In hindsight, it is quite clear that I began this study over forty-one years ago when, as a college undergraduate at Wesleyan University, I became chairperson of a combined student/faculty/administration committee charged with reexamining the entire academic program of the college. In my capacity as chair of this committee, I had the opportunity not only to review the range of course offerings of the college, but to discuss with student, faculty, and administrators the purposes and goals of various programs and majors. At that time David Riesman was engaged in his own study of higher education and was a regular visitor to the college.[110] I had the added opportunity not only to discuss the Wesleyan situation with him, but also to accompany him on numerous occasions when he visited other colleges and to participate in conferences and discussions regarding the status and future of higher education.

Since graduating from college, I realize, again in hindsight, that I have continued to pursue this project in a variety of different ways. Clearly, the most obvious is the fact that I elected to go on to graduate school and then spend my life as an academic. As an academic, I have had the opportunity through the years not only to participate on scores of different committees concerned with various aspects of higher education, but also to serve in a variety of leadership and administrative roles. These have included serving as a faculty senator, member, and chair of the faculty governance committee. In addition to chairing numerous other committees, I have been director of a number of different programs. assistant department chair, department chair, academic dean, and special assistant to the president. At the present time, I have returned full time to my academic role of professor of sociology, but have also been elected to another term as chair.

147

While the list of positions just detailed is perhaps longer than that of most academics, it is not unique. Nearly all academics serve on a variety of different committees and function as chair or in some equivalent leadership role during their academic careers. A good number also serve in higher administrative positions, such as a director of some program, associate provost, or dean.

In pondering the issues and writing this book, I have also drawn on other personal experiences. The first of these, while strictly speaking is a nonacademic role, has academic ties. I refer to my role as an active volunteer for my undergraduate college over the last forty years or so. As a fundraiser and alumni volunteer I have had the opportunity to listen to a wide range of opinions about higher education that I seldom if ever have heard as an academic. I have also been forced to examine the financial side of education from a range of different perspectives.

As an academic, even as an academic administrator, the main financial question I confront is, How am I going to get more resources? As a fundraiser, I have been put in the position of having to justify the money already spent. This has forced me to approach a number of issues from a different perspective. The role of volunteer has also provided me with a different type of access to administrators and other alumni than was available to me as a faculty member. When this volunteer role was combined with my role as parent of a college student, which it was for a number of years, it gave me access to other parents and a very different sort of access to current students.

Though I have learned a good deal about the dynamics of educational institutions in my roles of academic, academic administrator, and alumni volunteer, I have probably gained a better understanding of the unique nature of educational institutions through my various volunteer roles for other types of organizations. The other roles have provided me with a rich comparative stance. And through the years these other volunteer roles have been numerous. I served on the board and as an officer of a major synagogue for over ten years. I was also a board member and later president of a large Community Action Program in my hometown for a period of approximately six years. I was one of the early members and treasurer of a local Meals-on-Wheels program and served on its board for over ten years.

Interspersed with these various commitments, which themselves often overlapped, I served on an Educational Task Force for the city in which I lived, as board member and vice president of a fairly large neighborhood association, and a range of community and civic organizations. In nearly all of these situations, one of my primary responsibilities and concerns was normally the financial status and organizational structure of each establishment. What these various experiences have taught me and what I have found most interesting is the extent to which academic institutions function much like volunteer organizations.

Experiences in and of themselves can be valuable, but they are never assimilated in pure form, if in fact they ever exist in such form. All experiences are filtered through a complex of assumptions, biases, and pre-existing, though changing, schemata and frameworks. In the jargon of the academy, all facts are theoretically framed and informed. In my case, this theoretical framework has been formed and fashioned by my professional training and labors as a sociologist—more to the point in the present context, by my dual involvement and commitment to the sociology of knowledge and economic sociology.

As a sociologist of knowledge, I have had nearly a lifelong interest in studying and understanding the various ways people frame and define the world in which they live and how these different perspectives are shaped by people's social backgrounds and situations. As an economic sociologist interested mainly in markets, I am interested in understanding the various ways people attempt to assign monetary value to specific things and experiences. I am also interested in understanding how they also try to legitimate these economic values and convince themselves and others that the whole process is rational as well as legitimate. As a sociologist, I am particularly committed to understanding how social interactions and settings constrain these processes.

The extent to which all of these interests and concerns inform this study, I believe, is fairly obvious. What is perhaps not quite so obvious is the extent to which the study serves also to underscore the value of an informed broad sociological perspective on higher education. Obviously, higher education has been a subject of concern to sociologists for some time. Most studies done of higher education have probably been done by sociologists. Most of these sociologists, however, were sociologists of education. Education was and is their area of specialization. It isn't mine. I remain primarily interested in the sociology of knowledge and economic sociology.

What fascinates me, consequently, is not so much the actual educational policies and practices discussed in this book, but rather the ways that accounts and explanations are generated, disseminated, and propagated. It is in my roles as academic, alumnus, and citizen that I am primarily concerned with higher education. My wish, of course, is that the reader might find both issues of interest and importance. I clearly believe that American higher education, embodying as it does the best of the American dream, deserves our full and enthusiastic support. I similarly believe that sociology, as a way of understanding the world in which we live, is a valuable method that merits our constructive attention.

Notes

1. The concern with rising costs has been noted by many. See, for example, Charles T. Clotfelter, *Buying the Best* (Princeton: Princeton University Press, 1996), especially chapter 1, "The Problem of Rising Costs"; Donald Kennedy, *Academic Duty* (Cambridge: Harvard University Press, 1997), pp. 11–12; and Gallop survey figures reported in William F. Massy et al., *Resource Allocation in Higher Education* (Ann Arbor: University of Michigan Press, 1996), p. 18.

2. Tuition costs are averages drawn from a range of college catalogues for the years cited. The best comprehensive source for this data is the Department of Education's *IPEDS* (Integrated Post-Secondary Education Data System). My estimates are also based on data from the 1994 and 1995 *IPEDS* disks.

3. 1994 and 1995 *IPEDS* disks. See also Clotfelter, op. cit., and Massy et al.

4. Estimates of inflation are based primarily on the Composite Commodity Price Index for the years cited and other indicators from *How Much Is That in Real Money? A Historical Price Index for Use as a Deflator of Money Values in the Economy of the United States,* by John J. McCusker (Worcester, Mass.: American Antiquarian Society, 1992).

5. See Clotfelter for a discussion of the difficulty in comparing different types of institutions. The cost of different types of education, i.e., undergraduate, graduate, engineering, medicine, etc., varies as do certain auxiliary activities such as alumni relations, fundraising, etc.

6. Determining cost figures in this area is as much an art as a science. Different institutions use different guidelines in reporting their figures. Another major problem is the timeliness of the data. Probably the most recent systematic compilation of such figures found in Kent Halstead's *Higher Education Revenues & Expenditures* (Washington, D.C.: Research Associates of Washington, 1991) goes only to 1987, whereas the data in William F. Massy's 1996 edited volume *Resource Allocation in Higher Education* go only through 1994. In the text, I rely primarily on figures drawn from various institutional reports and the Department of Education 1994–1995 *IPEDS* data disk, which covers years 1990–1995.

7. This higher rate of inflation is recognized by the existence of the HEIP (the Higher Education Price Index), which has traditionally increased at a faster rate than the more widely cited CPI (Consumer Price Index). For a discussion of this issue, see Clotfelter, op. cit., pp. 34ff.

8. This is a key argument in Clotfelter's book, as its title indicates.

9. As noted in the text, I intend to review for the sake of comparison the educational expenditures incurred by different types of institutions. These comparisons will be followed by a more analytic analysis of these costs. Some readers may wish to skip directly to this latter analysis.

10. It might be argued that the semester at many institutions now runs only fifteen weeks. I have gone with the extra week since there is still normally a week or more of exams that do require the faculty.

11. Data drawn from *Military Training* pamphlet for FY 1996, published by the Office of the Under Secretary of Defense for Personnel and Readiness, and *Military Manpower Training 1997,* Report of the Department of Defense.

12. In the text I will use the terms "cost" and "expenditures" interchangeably.

13. As in the other cases, these figures are determined by dividing total reported costs by the number of students enrolled. This is admittedly an unsophisticated method of determining costs from a management perspective but in terms of dollars and cents is quite legitimate.

14. The American Society for Training and Development serves as an umbrella association for the training/educational programs of many companies.

15. Data drawn from *The Evaluation Guide to Executive Programs* (Fairfield, Iowa: Corporate University Press, 1994).

16. The American Society for Training and Development reports an average cost per employee for 1996 of those institutions reporting at approximately $1,500. Given that the targeted population for such training in most organizations seldom exceeds 25 percent, this works out to approximately $6,000 per trained employee. Figuring two weeks of training per year, on average, we come up with the same cost of $3,000 per week per person. Admittedly a gross estimate, but one that I would wager is fairly accurate. What needs to be taken into account here, however, is that most in-house training is basic, less expensive training.

17. *The World Bank Annual Report 1997,* p. 130. Total budget figure for training of $36,100,000 of total Research and Development Training budget of $77,400,000; oral communication from World Bank Staff.

18. In the annual report, a distinction is made between the 50 managers sent to Executive Development Programs (EDPs) at various leading business schools and academic institutions and the 180 persons sent through an "in-house" EDP program. Though this latter program is labeled an "in-house" program, it is also subcontracted to various leading business schools and academic institutions. The major difference seems to be that the in-house program is a six-week program that has its own curriculum, compared to the two- to four-week EDP programs that follow a more universal curriculum.

Even assuming that these external programs run for a full six weeks, and costing out each week for all programs at $4,000 per week, the total cost for these EDP programs would be less than $6,000,000 [(180 + 50) × 6 × $4,000 = $5,520,000]. Even doubling this figure, we are left with $24,000,000 to cover the other programs. With this money the World Bank sponsors three other types of programs: (1) approximately 150 technical workshops that in total service approximately 2,000 staff persons. These workshops run for different lengths of time, from only half a day up to five days; (2) 7 regional programs that service approximately 200 local staff persons; these programs last from one to two weeks; and (3) approximately 20 other training/educational programs that last from only a few days to up to a week.

Assuming a cost of $2,000 for each workshop participant, which is quite high considering the half-day to five-day length of these courses, and a $3,000 cost for each participant in the other weekly programs, we generate additional costs of $4,000,000, $600,000, and $1,500,000 (assumes an average attendance of twenty-five people per day in each program for a full week). Even doubling these figures and adding them to the earlier doubled figure for EDP courses, we end up with a total of less than $25,000,000, which is substantially less than the $36,000,000 budgeted.

Trying to convert these programs and costs into the equivalent college courses is nearly impossible since one is dealing with apples and oranges. Using the figures given previously, however, we ended up with weekly costs of $6,000 per person, which still leaves approximately one-third of the budget unspent. If we throw in the additional money, we end up with a weekly cost of just under $9,000. Multiplied by the normal college year of thirty-two weeks, this comes out to an annual cost of $270,000. This is more than the various military academies and we haven't built in the salaries that the various participants received while attending these courses. Some other companies, particularly consulting firms, based on descriptions of their programs, clearly spend as much. Unfortunately, these companies are hesitant to make their figures public. I know, because I've tried to get them.

19. *Education Statistics on Disk,* 1996 edition (Washington, D.C.: National Center for Educational Statistics, Department of Education).

20. Given modern computers and technology, it could be argued that these labor costs can be lowered. This is an issue that we will examine later.

21. Many faculty members, especially new faculty members, spend considerably more time than this. On the other hand, there are senior faculty members who manage to get away with less time. On average, however, the three-to-one figure is a fair generalization.

22. Various voluntary surveys of faculty have been done in recent years. Most of these surveys come up with an average work week of between forty-eight and sixty hours.

23. Faculty are also absent as a result of other types of leaves, but I am not including them here since, unlike sabbatical leaves, these leaves generally do not entail any salary payments to the faculty taking them.

24. Sabbatical leaves are normally awarded every seventh year, which results in a 15-percent loss of available faculty. I have then built in a 10-percent departmental loss for departmental administration and a 5-percent institutional loss. This comes to a total loss of 30 percent. In actuality, the figure is often higher.

25. Clotfelter, op. cit., pp. 144–145, uses a fringe benefit rate of approximately 23 percent for 1991/1992. This does not include FICA, however, and he notes that it continues to rise.

26. To be fair the 50-percent figure for buildings, etc., may be slightly overstated since these costs sometimes include costs for auxiliary buildings such as dorms, dinning halls, etc.

27. As indicated earlier, I believe $125,000 or even $250,000 per student per year is a much more accurate cost figure than the reported figure of $65,000, which fails to include all sorts of costs, allocated to other military budgets. While the figures presented in the text can be cited as revealing military extravagance, an equally good case can be made that they simply reveal how expensive the type of education provided by the various military academies is. Personally, I believe the latter judgment to be more accurate.

28. While the fringe packages tend to be more expensive, for simplicity's sake, we will stick with the $80,000 total compensation package. Average class size, however, needs to be reduced. The other ratios also need to be reduced because instruction tends to be more specialized, leading to more instructors per student, greater hierarchical structure generating a lower availability ration, and more numerous support staff. Reasonable estimates would be ACS = 16, TSCR = .4, FA = .6, FSR = .5. The most expensive difference, however, relates to the ratio of personnel costs and material costs. Where we used a ratio of .5 for the most endowed private colleges, a more appropriate, yet still conservative, ratio for the military academies would be .4. Plugging these figures into our formula, we get the following: ($80,000) ÷ (16 × .4 × .6 × .5) ÷ .4 = $104,166.66. Add on the cadet's salary plus fringe benefits, and spending $125,000 is easy. Moreover, one could easily run the cost up another $100,000 just by making one or two minor adjustments.

29. I am clearly not the first to suggest that many, if not most, institutions of higher education are actually underfunded. Howard R. Bowen makes this point in his 1980 book *The Cost of Higher Education* (San Francisco: Jossey-Bass, 1980) and others have since confirmed his calculations.

30. Figures based primarily on Composite Commodity Price Index for years cited and other indicators from *How Much Is That in Real Money? A Historical Price Index for Use as a Deflator of Money Values in the Economy of the United States,* by John J. McCusker (Worcester, Mass.: American Antiquarian Society, 1992).

31. See Kent Halstead's *Higher Education Revenues & Expenditures* (Washington, D.C.: Research Associates of Washington, 1991).

32. Figures drawn from *IPEDS* data disk. See also "For-Profit Higher Education," by Gordon C. Winston, *Change* (January/February 1999).

33. The distinction between direct and total costs will be discussed shortly.

34. See *Higher Education Revenues & Expenditures.*

35. In his *Resource Allocation in Higher Education,* Massy reports an inflation-adjusted compounded increase in tuition at private institutions between 1987 to 1993 of over 25 percent. An approximately similar increase is reported for public institutions, but whereas the increase is fairly evenly distributed for the private institutions, nearly all of the increase for public institutions occurred in the last three years.

36. The fact that the dean was a woman was not unrelated to the fact that the college was a women's college.

37. The history of public higher education, especially that of CUNY, clearly supports the position that many poorer students during this period completed their high school education and went on to college. Their total numbers were, however, comparatively small. More important, only a very few of these student aspired to attend elite private institutions.

38. Department of Education 1994 and 1995 *IPEDS* data disks.

39. *Higher Education Revenues and Expenditures.*

40. Department of Education 1994 and 1995 *IPEDS* data disks.

41. For one of the strongest attacks on administrative costs, see Barbara R. Bergmann, "Bloated Administration, Blighted Campuses," *Academe* (November/December 1991): 12–16.

42. *Buying the Best: Cost Escalation in Higher Education,* by Charles T. Clotfelter (Princeton: Princeton University Press, 1996).

43. We are caught up here in a little bit of an explanatory dilemma. The criticisms, which will be the focus of this chapter, have given rise to management changes that have themselves been criticized. To avoid confusion, the reader should understand that I am discussing the criticisms made of what might be called traditional academic management. I will later focus on various management innovations that were introduced to change things when we discuss the supposed "cures" recommended for higher education. While I am basically supportive of traditional academic administrative principles and practices, as will be seen later, I am quite critical of many modern forms. I might note here that America is not alone in experiencing such transformations in higher education. For an excellent overview of the British case, which also has a fair amount to say about the American case, see A. H. Halsey, *Decline of Donnish Dominion: The British Academic Professions in the Twentieth Century* (Oxford: Clarendon Press, 1992/1995).

44. While a number of different critics have voiced the criticism presented further on, the widely publicized comments by James F. Carlin, chair of the Massachusetts Board of Higher Education, are among the most extreme. See "The Ivory Tower Under Siege," by William H. Honan, *New York Times,* Section 4A (Education Life), January 4, 1998, pp. 33, 44, 46; and "A Take-No-Prisoners Approach to Changing Public Higher Education in Massachusetts," *Chronicle of Higher Education* (December 5, 1997).

45. See, for example, chapter 3, "Tenure Is a Necessary Condition of Academic Freedom," in George O'Brien's *All the Essential Half-Truths about Higher Education* (Chicago: University of Chicago Press, 1998) and the article on tenure, "Contracts Replace the Tenure Track for a Growing Number of Professors," *Chronicle of Higher Education* 44, no. 40 (June 12, 1998): 12–14.

46. Nearly all grants bring with them overhead money for the host institution. Such overhead can be as low as 10 percent, but it can also be nearly equal to the face value of the award.

47. The American Council on Education has played a lead role in this. The stated objective is to encourage institutions to emphasize and reward teaching at minimally the same level they reward research.

48. We will return to this aspect of the problem later when we begin to explore some of the cures that have been imposed on higher education during the last decade or so.

49. This is not to deny that most major research universities are interested in generating useful research findings. This aspect of their mission, however, tends to be more characteristic of their graduate rather than their undergraduate programs.

50. I should stress that I am discussing traditional governance systems, not some of the new systems being advocated as part of various recommended "cures," which will be examined later.

51. *In Search of History,* by Theodore H. White (New York: Harper and Row Publishers, 1978).

52. In remembering fondly the "good old days," it is important not to ignore their deficiencies. Despite the claims, most immigrants and native-born poor received little to no education until after the First World War. Moreover, while "night school" provided significant educational opportunities to numerous, often immigrant, individuals, overall educational access, especially to higher education and even more so to the prestigious private colleges and universities, was extremely restricted. On the other hand, night school was not only accessible, but, perhaps more important, because great efforts were made to maintain standards, its graduates were also respected, even if they were not treated as if they had graduated from Harvard.

53. From 1960 to 1995 the numbers of high school graduates between 16 and 24 years old enrolled in college went from 1,679,000 to 2,599,000, reflecting an increase of 45.1 percent of the cohort to 61.9 percent of the cohort. *Fact Book on Higher Education: 1997 Edition* (Phoenix: American Council on Education, Oryx Press, 1998).

54. While the percentage of male students enrolled in higher education increased just over 12 percent between 1960 to 1994, female enrollment increased by 67 percent. Black enrollment between 1980 to 1995 (there is no early data) increased 23 percent. See *Fact Book on Higher Education: 1997 Edition* (Phoenix: American Council on Education, Oryx Press, 1998)

55. This change has tended to be more specific to certain institutions, particularly public institutions servicing a greater percentage of new immigrants than was the norm thirty to forty years ago. The skill that many of these otherwise bright students often lack is a facility with the English language, since it is normally their second or even third language.

56. It is difficult to actually number the canon at any given time, but considering that literally tens of thousands of academic books are published each year, it takes little imagination to see how the *canon* in various disciplines has changed over a period of a few decades.

57. A number of factors have fed into this change. Perhaps the most significant, however, was passage of the Education Act of 1965, which for the first time established student learning as the essential outcome with which to judge federally funded educational programs. I want to thank Charles Karelis for pointing this connection out to me.

58. See, for example, the monthly newsletter put out by the New Caucus of CUNY. The New Caucus is an insurgent group within the larger Personnel Staff Congress (PSC) union of the University.

59. *The Closing of the American Mind,* by Allan Bloom (New York: Simon and Schuster, 1987).

60. For one interesting view on this subject, see *Education Still Under Siege,* by Stanley Aronowitz and Henry Giroux.

61. For those too young to know what the "gentleman's C–" was, it was the grade given to the well-bred student from the good, paying family who skipped many a class and did minimal work to get through the class. While most such students had the ability to do better, the work they submitted often deserved a failing grade. The C– grade was the tacit compromise for dealing with this situation. The student passed, but everyone knew that very little, if anything, had been learned.

62. I have on occasion equated going to college in these days to buying a ticket to the zoo. Tuition provided entrance to a new and exotic world where students could observe all sorts of strange people doing what they do. If they were bored by one performer or another they could move on, though they were generally required to read and remember at least some of the pamphlet material that was handed out in front of every cage. The "zoo" inmates, for their part, might elect to perform a little more energetically before a large and interested group of spectators, but for the most part they were indifferent. The only people, in fact, who they tended to take much interest in were colleagues and graduate students who shared their intellectual interests. This is clearly neither an accurate nor fair analogy in many ways, but on the other hand, it does catch the level of mutual disinterest that often did pervade.

63. This transformation of higher educational institutions into more student-centered institutions was further enhanced and legitimated by the Education Act of 1965, noted above in note 57.

64. While the price-cutting and revenue-enhancement efforts described in this chapter have been pursued to some degree by every academic administration, the new administrative class described in the next chapter has tended to be more aggressive than traditional administrations.

65. Administrators seldom if ever empower committees to determine what programs are to be eliminated or cut back. They normally only empower committees to recommend various options, and even then the administrator isn't limited to these options. If an administrator elects to go with a few of the recommended options and one or two of his or her own choosing, he or she can still claim to be acting in general accordance with the committee's recommendations.

66. In both cases, the initial decision to eliminate the department was presented as due to financial constraints. It was clear to those involved, however, that politically conservative administrations saw their fiscal crisis as an opportunity to eliminate what they saw to be a radical department. This was most clearly the case at Washington University where the Sociology Department was seen as embodying the views of its past chair, Alvin Gouldner. The ruling was reversed at Yale. It was implemented at Washington University.

67. We will have an opportunity to explore some of these options in part III.

68. This report, as well as the various responses from the individual colleges within the system, was widely circulated but never officially published. Copies can still be obtained from the central administrative office of the City University of New York.

69. It should be noted that this policy rapidly caused a formal union protest. The stated objective of the policy was to prohibit faculty members who had historically not taught additional courses from teaching an extra course during their last few years solely to increase their pensions. By not allowing faculty who had been teaching additional courses for years to do so during their last few years, however, the new policy served to decrease the pensions of faculty who, most would argue, were entitled to the higher pension since they had taught the extra courses for many years.

70. Assigning courses at most institutions is a chair's prerogative, but it is normally done in a collaborative manner. Most faculty members were able to get some reduction in their formal teaching load for extra large classes and various extra administrative activities. If the faculty member wanted to be assigned an overload class for

which he or she was paid, however, this person commonly wasn't given any reduction since such a reduction would make it difficult to justify overload pay.

71. Perhaps the most extreme example of this policy is that of the University of Phoenix, where 45,000 students are taught by a full-time faculty of only forty-five and legions of part-time adjuncts. We will have an opportunity to discuss the University of Phoenix in more detail later. Let it suffice to say for now, however, that the University of Phoenix makes no claim to offer a quality liberal arts and sciences education.

72. These figures are drawn from the 1994 and 1995 *IPEDS*.

73. The position presented in the text is drawn primarily from "What's Really Wrong with American Education—and What's Not," by Charles Karelis, *The College Board Review* 175 (Spring 1995).

74. Two factors that served to democratize the allocation of research grants were the 1965 Education Act, which, with its emphasis on student learning, created research opportunities for colleges and universities where teaching had always overshadowed research, and greater foundation concern with diversity and its impact on society as a whole and education more particularly. A number of highly diverse educational institutions, including a number of nonresearch institutions that had not been active in pursuit of traditional research grants, found themselves well positioned to receive these new grants.

75. See particularly the *Chicago Tribune* article of January 26, 1996, by Ron Glassman and Charles Leroux. A University of Rhode Island news release dated February 1, 1996, took issue with some of their figures. It argued that tuition subsidy was only $410 per student, rather than the $1,900 reported, and that the net research loss was only $9.3 million, not the $20 million reported. Clearly, the major point of my text, however, is supported.

76. A classic example of this has been the controversy generated by the gift of Perry Bass to Yale University to establish a Humanities Chair, which was rejected when the faculty concluded that Bass wanted to control the selection of the holder of the chair.

77. Some of the additional reasons for administrators to act in this fashion will be examined in the next chapter.

78. According to Karen Grassmuck, "Colleges Feel Effects of Economic Downturn in Student Aid, Endowment, Job Hunting," *Chronicle of Higher Education* 37, no. 14 (1990), between 1975 and 1985 administration grew 60 percent while faculty grew by 6 percent. In the last ten years, I would suggest this pattern has continued, if not become more skewed.

79. Some public institutions do not get caught up in this hassle since salaries, or at least a fairly limited salary range, are set by the state legislature.

80. When Peter Diamandopoulos was ousted from his job of past president of Adelphi University, due in no small part to his exorbitant salary and compensation package, claimed to be in excess of $800,000, he claimed the right, which he had arranged for himself while president, to a tenured professorship position at the rate of nearly $300,000 a year.

81. For a more general discussion of the negative impact that leadership changes can have on reorganization plans in higher education, see "How Colleges Cope When a President Leaves in the Midst of Restructuring," *Chronicle of Higher Education* (January 16, 1998): A41–A43.

82. See "Scholars Fear 'Star' System May Undercut Their Mission," *New York Times,* December 20, 1997, p. 1.

83. A doubling from 5 percent to 10 percent is consistent with Karen Grassmuck's figure when extended to the mid-'90s and adjusted for overall growth. I believe that this is actually a modest estimate for most institutions since there have been a few holdout institutions that have controlled their administrative growth.

84. It is extremely difficult to ascertain what these figures are, even though mean salaries are published quite regularly. One of the biggest problems is trying to decipher the various titles. *The Chronicle of Higher Education,* in its annual report, lists over 100 different administrative titles. The key comparison for me, however, is the comparison of salaries for the chief academic officer and the executive vice president, who is normally in charge of finances. While both positions normally pay considerably more than the faculty average, the executive vice president's average pay is more than the chief academic officer's in every type of institution.

85. There exists public information regarding the demographic characteristics of Ph.D. candidates, new Ph.D.s, and faculty in each academic discipline, which would constitute the larger pool from which a candidate pool would be drawn.

86. In advertising for a position, a cut-off date indicating when the review process will begin must be stated.

87. The extent to which many less-than-successful academics have moved into administrative positions in recent years is one of the great untold stories of American higher education.

88. Many of these organizations didn't even exist thirty years ago and those that did had much less visibility and influence than they do today.

89. It is important in this context to distinguish two very different meanings attached to the expression "post-tenure review." A growing number of institutions presently have some form of post-tenure review, in the sense that the activities of tenured faculty are reviewed and evaluated. Moreover, based on these reviews various actions can be and are taken. Whatever actions are taken, however, the faculty member's tenure is not in question. Some critics presently calling for "post-tenure review" have a very different idea in mind of what such reviews should be. For them, a post-tenure review should determine whether the faculty member maintains his or her tenure. This isn't a post-tenure review but a process that, in effect, does away with tenure.

90. I am clearly not alone in arguing that greater administrative centralization is counterproductive for higher education. Others have made the same point, though their reasons differ in various ways from those that I offer. For a very comprehensive case in favor of more decentralization, see *Research Allocation in Higher Education,* edited by Massy (Ann Arbor: University of Michigan Press, 1996).

91. This greater involvement with student activities is a by-product of the career patterns of many in the new administrative class, noted earlier. This career path is commonly characterized by a less-than-brilliant research career, leading to greater involvement in auxiliary and support activities that commonly entail more intensive interaction with students than normal classroom activities.

92. There are exceptions to this rule. A highly successful administratively supported mentoring program with which I am familiar is described in chapter 9. But, as will be noted in chapter 9, this program did not, and probably could not have, emerged from the administration.

93. I am indebted to my good friend Charles Olton, who after spending years in academia has recently turned his many skills to the world of symphony music, for this most informative comparative example.

94. While the expressions *college diploma* and *college degree* are often used interchangeably, they convey very different messages. Whereas the latter indicates completion of one step in an ongoing process, the former conveys the idea of completion and certification. The latter better describes the skill-oriented education required to do a job, whereas the former more accurately describes liberal education, which is intended to be only a step toward lifelong learning.

95. In both cases, it should be stressed, however, that we are talking about situations where the research demands are quite explicit. We are not discussing situations where faculty members are expected to engage in research in order to keep their own pedagogical skills well-honed but situations where the institution is expected to generate research findings for the larger community.

96. A number of these critics also seem perfectly happy to do away with liberal education.

97. What proved doubly disheartening was the fact that a number of faculty members who had previously been willing to teach courses similar to the world studies courses generated by this program refused to teach the new courses. Most of these faculty members had not been able to participate in this program, due to other commitments that prohibited them from attending the summer training program. They refused on the grounds that others had been rewarded for doing what they were expected to do for free. They would admit that they had done so for free before, but argued that once others had been paid extra for doing the same thing, they would not do so now.

98. To become eligible for the program, faculty members had to prepare a modest research proposal indicating what they intended to do and how they would use the student participants.

99. Because of the demand, we have been forced to establish a policy whereby you can only be funded once every four semesters.

100. It is perhaps misleading to attribute this strategy solely to "natural inclination." For over thirty-five years my area of research had been various types of economic markets, including all sorts of auctions. While the "market" strategies I favored may not have conformed to those embodied in the neoclassical economic model, they were clearly sympathetic with the strategies I had experienced in dealing with real markets.

101. The governing assumptions of the strategy presented in this section are similar in many ways to the strategy favored by Massy in his book *Research Allocation in Higher Education* (Ann Arbor: University of Michigan Press, 1996).

102. The University of Florida has been in the forefront of this effort. See "U. of Florida's 'Bank' Rewards Colleges That Meet Key Goals," *Chronicle of Higher Education* (February 26, 1999). One of the early pioneers in suggesting decentralizing economic decision making in higher education was Edward Whalen. His book, *Responsibility Centered Budgeting,* details his experiences at Indiana University in the late 1980s. For a general discussion see chapter 7, "Revenue Responsibility Budgeting," in *Research Allocation in Higher Education,* edited by Massy (Ann Arbor: University of Michigan Press, 1996).

103. Our report was submitted as an *interim* report because there were a number of issues stipulated in the charge that we could not resolve. In point of fact, however, our *interim* report de facto became our final report as changes in the administration lessened support for the project. This is, unfortunately, a fairly common occurrence in higher education where, as noted in chapter 6, there is increased administrative turnover.

104. The prisoners' dilemma is famous anomaly that emerged some time ago in the field normally referred to as Game Theory The gist of the problem lies in the following paradox. Two people are arrested and accused of committing a robbery. Each is told that if he confesses but his partner does not confess, he will receive a light sentence of only six months. His partner, however, will be sentenced to ten years in jail. On the other hand, if the partner confesses and he doesn't, the partner will get off in six months and he will be sentenced to ten years. If both refuse to confess, both will be sent to jail for a year based on a lesser charge. On the other hand, if both confess, both will be sent to jail for six years. The rational decision for both would seem to be to keep quiet. On the other hand, since each does better confessing no matter what the other one does—six months versus one year or six years versus ten years, the strategic decision for both is to confess. This means they end up going to jail for six years rather than six months. This "game" has been subject to intensive study and research. It clearly reveals, however, that without trust, rational actors can be expected to make decisions in which both suffer more than they would if they could trust each other.

105. See my *Auctions: The Social Construction of Values and Success* and *Survival on Wall Street: Understanding the Mind of the Market*.

106. The type of faculty-bashing by various self-proclaimed defenders of higher education exhibited in recent years, however, doesn't constitute a legitimate form of participation.

107. I will always remember the impact this difference had on my wife when she was first exposed to the American university system. Having completed her first degree in a well-known English university, she came to America to do additional graduate work. As an English graduate she was highly skilled in writing concise, literate essays. Her American professors, however, took her to task for failing to be more critical of the texts and for not presenting more of her own thoughts and ideas, practices that in England would have been considered presumptuous.

108. I am admittedly engaging in a bit of sophistry here, but I think that there is some substance to the point I am making. In this context, I might note that in America, *diploma* is used commonly in signifying completion of lower levels of education, where the issue is more one of having acquired certain fixed skills rather than having acquired a more open-ended ability.

109. As noted in the text, the tuition for full-paying students at most elite colleges and universities is often $10,000 less than the true costs. In contrast, tax support for most students attending public institutions is seldom more than $6,000 per year.

110. See "The Viability of the American College," by David Riesman and Christopher Jencks in *The American College,* edited by Nevitt Sanford (New York: John Wiley and Sons, 1962) and *Constraint and Variety in American Education* by David Riesman (Garden City, N.J.: Doubleday & Company, Inc., 1956, 1958).

References

American Council on Education. *Fact Book on Higher Education: 1997 Edition*. Phoenix, Ariz.: Oryx Press, 1998.

Anderson, Martin. *Impostors in the Temple*. Stanford, Calif.: Hoover Institution Press, 1996.

Aronowitz, Stanley, and Henry Giroux. *Education Still Under Siege*. Westport, Conn.: Bergin and Garvey, 1993.

Bergmann, Barbara R. "Bloated Administration, Blighted Campuses." *Academe* (November/December 1991): 12–16.

Bloom, Allan. *The Closing of the American Mind*. New York: Simon and Schuster, 1987.

Bowen, Howard R. *The Cost of Higher Education*. San Francisco, Calif.: Jossey-Bass, 1980.

Chancellor's Advisory Committee on Academic Program Planning. *The Goldstein Report*. Report by the City University of New York, 1992.

Clotfelter, Charles T. *Buying the Best*. Princeton, N.J.: Princeton University Press, 1996.

Department of Defense. *Military Manpower Training 1997*. Washington, D.C.: Report of the Department of Defense, 1998.

Department of Education. *IPEDS (Integrated Postsecondary Education Data System)*. Washington, D.C., 1994, 1995.

Grossman, Ron, and Charles Leroux. "Research Grants Actually Add to Tuition Costs, Study Reveals." *Chicago Tribune,* January 26, 1996.

Grassmuck, Karen. "Colleges Feel Effects of Economic Downturn in Student Aid, Endowment, Job Hunting." *Chronicle of Higher Education* 37, no. 14 (1990).

Halsey, A. H. *Decline of Donnish Dominion: The British Academic Professions in the Twentieth Century*. Oxford: Clarendon Press, 1992/1995.

Halstead, Kent. *Higher Education Revenues & Expenditures*. Washington, D.C.: Research Associates of Washington, 1991.

Healy, Patrick. "A Take-No-Prisoners Approach to Changing Public Higher Education in Massachusetts." *Chronicle of Higher Education* (December 5, 1997): A41–42.

Honan, William H. The Ivory Tower Under Siege." *New York Times,* January 4, 1998, Section 4A (Education Life).

Karelis, Charles. "What's Really Wrong with American Education—And What's Not," *The College Board Review* 175 (Spring 1985).

Kennedy, Donald. *Academic Duty.* Boston, Mass.: Harvard University Press, 1997.

Leroux, Charles. University of Rhode Island news release dated February 1, 1996.

Lively, Kit. "U. of Florida's 'Bank' Rewards Colleges That Meet Key Goals." *Chronicle of Higher Education* (February 26, 1999): A35–36.

Massy, William F., et al. *Resource Allocation in Higher Education.* Ann Arbor: University of Michigan Press, 1996.

Military Manpower Training Report: FY 1997, Office of the Under Secretary of Defense for Personnel and Readiness: Department of Defense.

Military Training: FY 1996, Office of the Under Secretary of Defense for Personnel and Readiness: Department of Defense.

McCusker, John J. *How Much Is That in Real Money? A Historical Price Index for Use as a Deflator of Money Values in the Economy of the United States.* Worcester, Mass.: American Antiquarian Society, 1992.

Mercer, Joyce. "How Colleges Cope When a President Leaves in the Midst of Restructuring." *Chronicle of Higher Education* (January 1998): A41–43.

O'Brien, George. *All the Essential Half-Truths about Higher Education.* Chicago: University of Chicago Press, 1988.

Riesman, David. *Constraint and Variety in American Education.* Garden City, N.J.: Doubleday & Company, Inc., 1956/1958.

Riesman, David, and Christopher Jencks. "The Viability of the American College." In *The American College,* edited by Nevitt Sanford. New York: John Wiley and Sons, 1962.

Scott, Janny. "Scholars Fear 'Star' System May Undercut Their Mission." *New York Times,* December 20, 1997, p.1.

Shumar, Wesley. *College for Sale: A Critique of the Commodification of Higher Education,* London & Washington, D.C.: Falmer Press, 1997.

Smith, Charles W. *Auctions: The Social Construction of Values,* New York: Free Press, 1989. (Paperback edition: University of California Press, 1990.)

Smith, Charles W. *Success and Survival on Wall Street: Understanding the Mind of the Market.* Boulder: Rowman & Littlefield, 1999.

Whalen, Edward. *Responsibility Centered Budgeting: An Approach to Decentralized Management for Institutions of Higher Education.* Bloomington: Indiana University Press, 1991.

White, Theodore H. *In Search of History.* New York: Harper and Row Publishers, 1978.

Winston, Gordon C. "For Profit Higher Education." *Change* (January/February 1999).

World Bank staff oral communication. *The World Bank Annual Report 1997.*

The Evaluation Guide to Executive Programs. Fairfield, Iowa: Corporate University Press, 1994.

Wilson, Robin. "Contracts Replace the Tenure Track for a Growing Number of Professors." *Chronicle of Higher Education* (June 12, 1998): A12–14.

Index

About the Author

CHARLES W. SMITH is presently professor and chair of the sociology department at Queens College, CUNY, where he has taught since 1965, and a member of the doctoral program in sociology at the CUNY Graduate School. He received his B.A. degree from Wesleyan University and his M.A. and Ph.D. from Brandeis University; he has been a visiting scholar at Nuffield College, Oxford, in 1979–1980 and Wesleyan University in 1987–1988. From 1991 through 1996, he served as dean of faculty for the social sciences at Queens College. During the academic year 1996–1997, he served as a special assistant to the president for special projects. Most of his publications, which include *Success and Survival on Wall Street: Understanding the Mind of the Market* (1999); *Auctions: The Social Construction of Value* (1989); *The Mind of the Market: A Study of Stock Market Philosophies, Their Uses, and Their Implications* (1981); and *The Critique of Sociological Reasoning: An Essay in Philosophic Sociology* (1979), as well as numerous articles and chapters, are in the areas of economic sociology and general theory. During the last seven years he has been awarded two Ford Foundation grants as well as a FIPSE award to support various innovative projects. Since 1984 he has been the editor of *Journal for the Theory of Social Behaviour*, published by Basil Blackwell, Oxford, England. He remains interested and committed to a wide range of community, civic, and educational organizations, most of which he has been associated with for many years. He is married and the father of two grown children.